Giant Perennials

Giant Perennials

Susan Berry

Photography by Steve Wooster

FIREFLY BOOKS

A FIREFLY BOOK

Published by Firefly Books Ltd., 2003

Publisher Cataloging-in-Publication Data (U.S.)
(Library of Congress Standards)
Berry, Susan.
Giant perennials / Susan Berry.—1st ed.
[128] p.: col. ill.: photos.; cm.
Includes index.
Summary: Illustrated guide to large-sized perennials (over 5 ft./3 m. in height) for the garden plus tips on cultivation and design
ISBN 1-55297-749-8
ISBN 1-55297-712-9 (pbk.)
1. Foliage plants. 2. Perennials. I. Title.
635.9/32 21 CIP SB431.B47 2003

National Library of Canada Cataloguing in Publication
Berry, Susan, 1944-
Giant perennials / Susan Berry.
Includes index.
ISBN 1-55297-749-8 (bound)
ISBN 1-55297-712-9 (pbk.)
1. Perennials. I. Title.
SB434.B47 2003 635.9'32 C2002-902720-9

First published in the United States in 2003 by
Firefly Books (U.S.) Inc.
P.O. Box 1338, Ellicot Station
Buffalo, New York 14205

First published in Canada in 2003 by
Firefly Books Ltd.
3680 Victoria Park Avenue
Toronto, Ontario M2H 3K1

Senior Editors Claire Wedderburn-Maxwell and Clare Churly
Editor Jennie Halfant
Designer Ruth Hope
Photographer Steve Wooster
Plant Consultant Anthony Lord
Illustrator Ian Sidaway

Reproduction by Classicscan Pte Ltd in Singapore
Printed and bound by Imago in Singapore

Contents

Introduction

I have only a very small garden, some 50ft (15m) long and a mere 18ft (5.5m) wide, in which I grow a disproportionate number of very large perennials (although nothing like all of those that are featured in this book). My interest began when I first edited books written by Anthony Paul, a garden designer from New Zealand, whose passion for large plants and for large drifts of large plants characterize his work.

Until then, like almost everyone else, I had been more swayed by flower color than foliage power, and I saw the art of garden design as being more like painting than sculpture. Anthony has an unrivaled sense of space and place, however, and his own garden was a revelation to me, concentrating as it does on foliage plants, many of them giants. Anthony's work is imbued by a completely different sense of scale from that of any other garden designer whose work I have seen. Although it works brilliantly in enormous gardens like his own, it also translates even more effectively into very small gardens, where the effect is magical. Far from making the gardens seem smaller, these large plants, often planted in big groups, create a feeling of relaxed spaciousness.

Obviously, the success of any planting scheme relies on a mixture of heights and plant forms, but the fact that these giants are perennials, and therefore are around for only part of the year, creates a more exciting dimension in the garden—they bring a sense of the unexpected and of great surprise. Were the height achieved by shrubs alone, the picture would be more or less permanent throughout the year, with the obvious advantage that you would look out on the same landscape all year round, but the disadvantage that there would be no element of change or progress.

It is precisely the ability of nature to astound and delight us (and, it must be admitted, also to disappoint us!) that makes gardening such a fascinating and all-absorbing occupation. Nothing amazes and delights us more than to watch a plant grow before our eyes in a very short space of time, as anyone who has grown an amaryllis (*Hippeastrum*) or spider plant (*Chlorophytum comosum*), for example, will testify!

Many subtropical perennials are among the fastest growing plants, but those of us who

garden in temperate climates and do not have greenhouses must concentrate on hardy or half-hardy plants. A few of the more tender giants are included in this book, but the majority of those included will survive light frosts, even if they won't survive the coldest climates.

About this book

The perennials included in this book are those that reach a height of around 5ft (1.5m) or more, although the term "giant" is somewhat arbitrary.

The directory of plants offers you a wide range of plants of this height for a wide range of conditions. If you check the symbols at the top of each entry, you can work out quite quickly which ones are likely to be suitable for the conditions in your garden (damp, dry, sun, or shade). They also give you some helpful clues about care. At the foot of each entry are some suggested planting combinations. Naturally, not all of these are giant, since the aim of any planting scheme is to vary the heights.

Above: Contrasting texture and form add interest to any garden. Here, giant rhubarb (Gunnera manicata) *leaves provide a foil for delicate, slender grasses.*

Below: In this late summer border, composed almost entirely of giant perennials in great drifts, silver grass (Miscanthus), *feather grass* (Stipa), *thistles* (Onopordum), *asters and Joe Pye weed* (Eupatorium) *combine in a rich tapestry of color.*

DESIGNING WITH GIANT PERENNIALS

Planning planting schemes

The impact that giant perennials make is, understandably, huge, but it is important to keep in mind that because most of them are herbaceous perennials and die down in winter, the impact is relatively short-lived (even though many of them also have handsome foliage, which can extend their season of interest from late spring to the first frosts of autumn).

Another important consideration to take into account are the effects of climate, soil, and location. A perennial that might perform like a giant in the right conditions probably will not do so in less suitable ones, and the expected 5ft (1.5m) of growth may fail to materialize so that you are left with a somewhat puny performer.

When you design with giant perennials, work out where and how you want the impact and make sure that you have some permanent structural plants in place for the remaining months of the year. It always pays to have a balance of evergreen and deciduous plants (be they trees, shrubs, climbers, or perennials). In a small garden, you do not necessarily want your star performing giants to block your view of their smaller, but no less attractive, cousins.

Color is an important element in planning all planting schemes, but rather than try to be too precise, the simplest approach is to go for either cool color schemes (whites, pale blues, lemon yellows, pale pinks, pale mauves) or hot colors (reds, strong pinks, buttery yellows, oranges, strong warm blues, purples). Leave the very precise color planning to the experts. By planning a palette based on "tone" (when everything has much the same degree of color saturation) you prevent any one plant from leaping forward and dominating the scheme.

The most important place for big perennials is at the back of the border, but not everyone has traditional perennial borders; these days drifts of a single plant, or much larger plantings of individual plants that are all the same height, have become popular, thanks in some degree to the planting inspiration of Dutchman Piet Oudolf. Other useful places for big perennials are to mark the corner of a border or to provide some kind of screen, so that not all of the garden can be viewed at one glance.

In my own small city garden I have Chinese rhubarb (*Rheum palmatum* 'Atropurpureum') in a

bog garden at the back of a pond, which is actually more or less in the center of the garden and one-third of the way down it. It forms a giant screen from late spring to mid-autumn, making the garden seem incredibly lush and successfully masking the view to the end of the garden, so that it appears larger than it is. In another bog garden near to it is a large clump of bamboo, which also provides a successful screen; however, the light, delicate, feathery foliage provides an excellent contrast with the huge hand-shaped leaves of the ornamental rhubarb. (As an aside, make sure you buy "Atropurpureum;" I made the mistake of buying "Ace of Spades," which looks similar, but is altogether less riveting, with less-serrated leaves and no interesting reddish coloring.) At the far end, under trees, I have a thicket of plume poppies (*Macleaya*), the golden plumes of which catch the sun as it disappears down over the horizon. Grasses do similar service, their delicate flowerheads catching the light in the most captivating way.

My garden is shaded by a huge cider gum (*Eucalyptus gunnii*), which means that I must grow shade-loving plants, of which, fortunately, a good few are large (no doubt evolving to cope with low light levels by reaching closer to the sun). Those with a sunnier plot have a wider palette of plants to choose from, many of which will look very different. Just as my bog garden favors moisture-loving, large-leafed plants, you may have thin, dry, gravelly soil on which to grow Mediterranean plants with silvery leaves and bright flowers.

Above: In this very different, small, wild garden, giant perennials include mulleins (Verbascum *spp.) and common foxgloves* (Digitalis purpurea).

Below: This handsome border features Helianthus annuus, *'Lemon Queen', orange coneflower* (Rudbeckia fulgida) *and* Persica amplexicaulis *'Atrosanguineum'.*

Planting for damp conditions

Those plants that originate in moist areas—alongside streams and lakes or in very wet climatic conditions—are those most suitable for the damp areas of your own garden, whether they are naturally occurring damp areas or bog gardens of your own making. If you do not have naturally damp conditions, there is nothing to prevent you from creating them, and one of the advantages of doing so is that it lends great variety to the plants and therefore greater interest. Ideally, a bog garden should look natural, so the best places are next to a pond or in a naturally low-lying area of the garden. Some moisture lovers prefer full sun, some prefer partial shade, so either situation is fine. To create a bog garden, use a plastic liner buried to a depth of 3ft (1m) or so, and puncture a few holes in the base so that it drains, but not as freely as the soil in the rest of the garden. The aim is to keep the soil moist but not waterlogged.

Among the many really large-leafed plants that enjoy damp conditions are the huge giant rhubarb (*Gunnera manicata*), which is not fully hardy and is one of the true giants—it can grow to 8ft (2.5m) or more tall and wide—and the smaller but rather similar Chinese rhubarb. Other good large-leafed candidates for bog gardens are rodgersias and leopard plants (*Ligularias*). Many bamboos and astilbes have more finely divided leaves, while those with sword-shaped leaves include the water irises (*Iris laevigata*), which will grow well in water up to 6in (15cm) deep.

Although hostas are not giant perennials, their leaves are large enough to make excellent companion plants for some of the really big plants. In particular, the bluish-green *Hosta sieboldiana* var. "Elegans" has large, handsome clumps of heavily ribbed leaves and does best in damp conditions.

*Right: In this damp border, a good combination of foliage forms prevail, with the variegated sword-shaped leaves of the pale yellow iris (*Iris pseudacorus 'Variegata'*), the rounded leaves of a Chinese rhubarb (*Rheum palmatum*) and the silver-edged leaves of a hosta (*Hosta crispula*).*

Below: With their handsome, rounded leaves and spires of pink flowers, rodgersias take center place around a pool.

Planting for dry conditions

Even in areas with ample rainfall, there may be parts of your garden with drier soil—in the shadow of a wall, for example, or under trees. For these areas, it is a question then of choosing plants that naturally prefer these conditions.

Many of the plants that have learned to adapt to very dry conditions have silvery foliage, usually as a consequence of the leaves being covered with downy hairs that help to limit moisture loss. Others have very waxy leaves that hold in moisture, some of them have fine and needle-like hairs in an attempt to reduce evaporation. As a consequence, plants for dry gardens have an overall similarity of appearance that helps to unify the planting scheme. Part of the secret of successful garden design is to pay attention to the dictates of nature, because you will not find unfortunate clashes of style in natural surroundings.

Among the biggest plants that cope well with dry conditions are some good foliage plants, including many of the thistles with their filigree, almost metallic, grayish-blue foliage, such as cotton thistle (*Onopordum acanthium*) and sea holly (*Eryngium agavifolium*). Spurges (*Euphorbia*) with their waxy, narrow leaves, also do well in dry areas.

Other star large performers for dry conditions in full sun are torch lilies (*Kniphofia* spp.), sweet fennel (*Foeniculum*) and giant fennel (*Ferula communis*), the truly statuesque mullein (*Verbascum* spp.), with its large, wonderfully felted, silver-gray leaves and spires of yellow flowers, and the scented evening primrose (*Oenothera* spp.) with its saucer-shaped, pale yellow flowers.

There are many grasses that enjoy dry, prairie-like conditions, too. Some of the plants that prefer moist conditions will tolerate a degree of dryness—yarrow (*Achillea* spp.), Monkshood (*Aconitum* spp.), and Japanese anemones (*Anemone* × *hybrida*), for example. For those plants that can suffer if the soil becomes too dry, use a mulch to retain as much moisture as possible. Choose between organic mulches, which help feed the soil but need frequent replacing, and inorganic ones, such as gravel, which are more or less permanent.

Above: Silvery thistles (Eryngium giganteum) *make a good back of the border plant. The colors combine well with blues, mauves and pinks.*

Above: Red-hot-pokers (Kniphofia) *create a vibrant splash of color for a hot color-themed border.*

Left: One of the island beds in this gravel garden features mulleins (Verbascum), *blue oat grass* (Helictotrichon sempervirens), *spurge* (Euphorbia) *and foxgloves* (Digitalis) *with smaller perennials.*

Planting for shade

You will have to reconcile yourself to the fact that, in general, shade-loving plants will be less brightly colored than sun-loving plants. Those plants that thrive in shade tend to have large leaves and pale, small, or insignificant flowers. There are good botanical reasons for this, which you do not need to absorb, but it is no good thinking that you are going to have the vibrant color of a Mediterranean-style garden in ground that is predominantly shaded. However, you will get the opportunity to have some wonderful foliage plants, and you can begin to appreciate the joys of form and texture (an altogether more grown-up experience in design terms!). Nevertheless, foliage can itself come in a surprising variety of colors.

The big, pleated leaves of false hellebore (*Veratrum*), the plate-sized leaves of many rodgersias, the leaves of large hostas, like *Hosta sieboldiana* var. "Elegans" (not a giant, but worth growing alongside them, and certainly a giant among hostas), the handsome, hand-shaped leaves of Chinese rhubarb (extolled earlier) are just a few of the joys that you can experience in a predominantly shady border or garden. Many of the ferns, too, with their delicately branched and arching fronds, prefer shade. In moist, shady conditions plant the wood fern (*Dryopteris* spp.) or ostrich fern (*Matteuccia* spp.).

It is worth remembering that not all shade is the same. It varies in degree, and the conditions can vary from dry (such as occurs on the leeside of walls and under large trees) to damp (alongside streams, for instance, and in boggy areas of ground).

A perennial that will romp away in dry shade may well stagnate in waterlogged conditions and vice versa. If you look at the natural habitat of a plant (where it thrives in the wild), this will give you a good clue, but it is not an absolute guide, because many different species have widely different needs, having learned to adapt very successfully in different regions of the world.

If you want to vary the planting scheme more than conditions permit, use containers. Suggestions are given on pages 28–9. Most sun-loving plants will cope with shade for a limited period (a couple of months) before they start to fail, and so you can introduce a little temporary color in pots for the summer months if you wish.

*Opposite: Skunk cabbage (*Lysichiton americanus*), while not a tall plant, rapidly produces large clumps of eye-catching leaves, with bright yellow flower spathes in spring.*

*Left: Plume poppies (*Macleaya cordata*) catch the light in this woodland garden.*

*Below: Foxgloves (*Digitalis*) from the Excelsior Group, shaded by palms, combine to make a stunning display in this New Zealand garden.*

Planting for sun

The great majority of plants grow best in full sun and will put on most growth if they are given adequate sunlight, moisture, and food. However, you must be aware that this is not true of plants that have evolved in habitats such as woodlands. These plants will quickly scorch and shrivel if they are exposed to the full glare of the summer sun. Not all the plants that are sun lovers prefer drier conditions, however, and those that grow by stream sides, for example, like both sunshine and moisture. Others, particularly those originating in Mediterranean regions or on hillsides, like free-draining soil and have evolved to cope with drought; these plants often have leaves that are covered in fine silver hair or a waxy coating to help reduce moisture loss.

In general, however, if your garden is sunny, you may have so many choices that it will make the designing and planning decisions surprisingly difficult; the wide selection may be your undoing. With a wide range of plants at your disposal, you need to start thinking of themes for your plants so that you achieve some kind of unity.

It is always a good idea to include some plants for foliage and texture, rather than just flower color. Many of the grasses, such as silver grass (*Miscanthus* spp.) and moor grass (*Molinia*

Above: If you position grasses facing west, the dying sun will catch their seedheads, which glint attractively in the light.

Right: A sea of purple alliums brings this summer border to life.

spp.), are excellent for this purpose, as are those with sword-shaped leaves, such as irises and yuccas.

One of the best solutions in a very sunny garden with a low average rainfall is to create a gravel garden, so that the gravel acts as a much needed mulch, preventing the roots of the plants from drying out.

Beth Chatto has created an exceptionally successful gravel garden in the very dry climate where she lives. In it, giant perennials form the backbone of the island beds, where they are surrounded by smaller perennials. Her choice for the large perennials for full sun includes mulleins, ornamental onions (*Allium*), thistles, purple verbena (*Verbena bonariensis*), evening primroses, and grasses. However, before planting, she put a great deal of effort into creating really fertile soil, which helps to hold what little moisture there is. The gravel acts as a mulch, which retains moisture and helps to keep roots cool (as well as suppressing weeds).

In sunny gardens, it is worth your while positioning tall plants where they will catch the light in the setting sun. The big thistles and tall grasses are excellent for this purpose, and the effect helps to lighten the plants, making them look more ethereal.

Planting for color

Producing the kind of carefully graded color schemes favored by Gertrude Jekyll is probably beyond the scope of most gardeners, as it requires a very good knowledge of plants, and an equally good eye for color values. The wrong shade of any one color will throw off the whole scheme.

It is better to be less ambitious and to aim for color harmonies that create a pleasing, unified effect. The simplest way to do this is to divide the color palette into those colors that are warm or hot and those that are cool and to plan your planting scheme accordingly. Just to make things complicated, the color blue, which most of us would assume would be in the "cool" spectrum, can be cool or hot. When there is plenty of yellow in its makeup, it becomes "cool," but with plenty of red in its make-up it becomes "hot." By and large, the cool colors tend to be the paler hues, and the hot colors are the stronger intense ones.

Hot color schemes

The hot colors include those like rich buttery yellow, strong oranges, reds of any description, bright pinks, strong purples and mauves, and those blues that tend to sing out as the light falls. Many of the flowers with these color values tend to be sun-lovers, so "hot" color schemes are almost always for sunny gardens.

This kind of color theme looks particularly good in gravel gardens, which tend to have a predominance of Mediterranean plants, many of which have silvery foliage and brightly colored flowers. You can opt for a color range that combines toning shades—for example, purples, reds and pinks, or yellows, oranges, and reds—or you can combine all the strong, hot colors together in a mixed display of strongly contrasting hues.

Strongly clashing colors have become increasingly popular in recent times; bright red dahlias and purple Verbena bonariensis *make an eye-catching combination.*

An equally-strong clashing scheme, with the pinkish-purples of knotweed (Persicaria), *Joe Pye weed* (Eupatorium), *and the brilliant yellows of orange coneflower* (Rudbeckia fulgida).

In recent years, schemes with contrasting hot colors have become very popular, their virtues extolled by youthful television gardening hosts and some of the experimental contingent of more established gardeners, such as Christopher Lloyd and Sarah Raven. Hot mauves with strong reds or deep purples with buttery yellows make a vivid impression. With these strong colors, it is best not to go for overkill but to limit the planting scheme to a contrast of, say, a couple of colors. You do not have to make these contrasts with other giants, simply use the giants at the back and plants of slightly smaller stature in front of them. A bed of the purple verbena could combine with bright pink and red cosmos or with dark red dahlias, for example.

To create a "hot" scheme, you do not have to concentrate solely on the hottest colors, but avoid white at all costs. It tends to break up the overall effect, and stands out too dramatically against the "blocked" effect of the warmer colors.

BORDER OF HOT COLORS

Aster novae-angliae 'Andenken an Alma Pötschke' – red
Baptisia australis – dark blue
Delphinium 'Bruce' – purple blue
Eremurus 'Firecracker' – orange
Fritillaria imperialis – orange or yellow
Helenium 'Goldrausch' – bright yellow
Helenium 'Septemberfuchs' – dark orange
Kniphofia 'Samuel's Sensation' – scarlet
Ligularia stenocephala – yellow
Lilium superbum – orange
Meconopsis grandis – bright blue
Primula florindae – bright yellow
Rudbeckia laciniata 'Hortensia' – bright yellow
Verbena bonariensis – purple

Cool color schemes

The paler colors tend to be the cool ones—the light greens and powder blues, lemony yellows, pale pinks, pale mauves, and, of course, white (which is not actually a color but is treated as one). Planted together, they create a soft, appealing palette that gives the garden a relaxed and spacious feel; and because the shades of the different colors are soft and muted, the overall effect is harmonious without being dull. A pale, cool color theme will help to make a small garden feel more spacious, and pale colors stand out well against a dark evergreen backdrop, such as yew (*Taxus*).

The feathery foliage of grasses looks particularly attractive combined with a cooler color theme, and it is well worth punctuating clumps of flowering perennials with a repeating motif of a handsome grass, such as Chinese silver grass (*Miscanthus sinensis*) or purple moor grass (*Molinia caerulea*).

When it comes to planning the planting scheme for shady areas, you will find that you are probably limited to the cooler colors, simply because brightly colored flowers do not flourish in low light levels. One of the simpler single-color themes to create for sun or shade is an all-white one, in part because there is a good variety of white-flowered plants, and because you do not have to balance color values.

Among the big white flowering plants for the back of an all white border are colewort (*Crambe cordifolia*), Japanese anemone (*Anemone* × *hybrida* "Géante des Blanches"), *Astilbe* "Professor van der Wielen" and the white foxglove (*Digitalis purpurea* f. *albiflora*). You can create mixed borders (taking care to combine plants that enjoy similar conditions) or you can create single drifts of one plant. Those that self-seed or colonize well are ideal for this purpose: Japanese anemones spread fairly quickly in the right conditions, as do fox-gloves, although the seedlings may not take root.

*Left: A softly colored palette has been created with white mullein (*Verbascum lychnitis*), the foliage of plume poppies (*Macleaya*),* Sidalcea, *bee balm (*Monarda*) and phlox.*

*Above: The cool white spires of foxtail lily (*Eremurus himalaicus*) stand out above a mixed palette of pinks and mauves created by rock roses (*Cistus*) and columbines (*Aquilegias*).*

*Below: The pale yellow flowers of mulleins (*Verbascum *'Gainsborough') are set off by the dark blue of the bugloss (*Anchusa*) behind.*

BORDER OF COOL COLORS

Allium giganteum – pale mauve
Anemone × hybrida – white or pale pink
Angelica archangelica – greenish yellow
Aruncus dioicus – white
Astilbe grandis – white
Campanula lactiflora – white, blue or violet
Crambe cordifolia – white
Cynara cardunculus – silver foliage, mauve
Delphinium 'Fanfare' – light mauve
Digitalis purpurea 'Sutton's Apricot' – pale apricot
Epilobium angustifolium var. *album* – white
Galega × hartlandii 'Lady Wilson' – mauve and white
Leucanthemella serotina – white
Lilium candidum – white
Oenothera biennis – pale yellow
Ostrowskia magnifica – pale blue

Planting for foliage

Most of us, particularly when we are novice gardeners, are attracted initially by the flowering qualities of plants: the bigger and brighter the flowers, the better. As we spend more time gardening, however, we begin to realize that what really creates the essential quality of a garden—its texture, shape, and character—is the foliage, and the more closely we observe it, the more varied and interesting it appears. Although gardeners are often obsessed with planting for color, the way in which leaves contrast or harmonize is the "glue" that holds any garden design together. Unlike flowers, which are ephemeral, the foliage is there all year round on evergreen plants and for the larger part of the year on deciduous ones.

As far as giant perennials are concerned, it is the "giant" quality of the leaves that often turns them into star performers. Ask anyone what the flowers of giant rhubarb look like and they will be hard pressed to tell you, but almost any gardener can recognize the huge, 5ft (1.5m) wide leaves. When you are thinking about foliage effects, consider how well the leaves of plants will combine. Contrasts of shape, color and foliage texture are vital, as are contrasts of growth habit: stiffly upright, as with yuccas, or delicately arching, as with many grasses, for example. Planting schemes are most successful when the various attributes are taken into account and used to paint a wider picture.

When you start to concentrate on foliage you quickly realize just how many different shades of green there are and how to use these variations in hue to add more life to the garden. A garden composed entirely of foliage plants with dark, glossy leaves would look very heavy and dull. But combine small, dark, glossy leaves with large, soft, apple green leaves, include the occasional grass with its fine, arching leaves, and back it with a plant with amazingly silvered, toothed leaves, and the picture immediately comes to life.

Right: The huge leaves of giant rhubarb make a wonderful contrast with the sword-shaped foliage of phormiums and cordylines.

*Below: In a drier setting, a mixture of grasses present a different foliage screen, with feather reed grass (*Calamagrostis x acutiflora *'Karl Foerster') and* Miscanthus sinensis.

Planting through the seasons

Herbaceous perennials make their mark from late spring and early summer to late autumn. In the winter months, only those that are evergreen (which are a small minority) are still in evidence, so your planting plan encompasses roughly two-thirds of the year.

The late spring performers in the garden are predominantly bulbs, but the giants among bulbs all perform slightly later, from very late spring to midsummer. Among these are giant lily (*Cardiocrinum giganteum*), with its giant spires of tubular white flowers in early summer; Crown Imperial Fritillary (*Fritillaria imperialis*) with its striking, orange crown-like blooms in late spring to early summer; ornamental onion (*Allium giganteum*) with its huge starry heads of purple flowers in early summer; and finally, the richly fragrant, large lilies in full summer. There are also two early-flowering clematis: *C. armandii* and *C. montana*, of which *C. armandii* is the earlier.

Among the earlier summer perennials are *Aruncus, Astilbe, Baptisia, Campanula, Euphorbia*, evening primroses and King Solomon's seal (*Polygonatum* spp.). Shortly afterward come *Achillea, Coreopsis, Crambe, Cynara, Delphinium*, foxgloves (*Digitalis* spp.), sea hollies (*Eryngium* spp.), torch lilies, *Meconopsis, Scabiosa, Salvia, Thalictrum*, and *Verbascum*.

To take you through to late summer, there are a number of plants with long flowering seasons, including *Achillea, Anemone × hybrida, Astilbe, Campanula, Coreopsis, Echinacea, Echinops, Eryngium, Eupatorium, Galega, Kniphofia, Phlox, Rudbeckia, Salvia*, and *Scabiosa*. In addition, there are those that flower in late summer and early autumn, including *Aster, Boltonia, Clematis tangutica, Helianthus, Helenium, Inula, Lespedeza*, and *Persicaria*.

Grasses will present a long-standing display from late spring through to late autumn or even later, and help to produce a feeling of continuity.

A late summer border, its autumnal shades formed from grasses, like silver grass (Miscanthus) *and feather grass* (Stipa) *combining with the pinkish purples of* Persicaria *and Joe Pye weed* (Eupatorium).

In summer the mulleins (Verbascum), *ornamental onions* (Allium), *and bearded irises combine in an exquisitely toned palette of pinks and purples.*

In early summer in this damp garden, the bright yellow flowers of Tibetan cowslip (Primula florindae) *bring the foliage display of big grasses and large-leaved ligularias to life.*

Giant perennials in containers

The idea of growing giant perennials in containers might seem to be a contradiction in terms, but it is surprising how much a few really large plants in pots can contribute to a garden. One of the most appealing aspects of these big perennials is that they can do their stuff in one or two seasons at most, while you would have to wait several years for a containered shrub to get to such heights.

If you wish, there is nothing to stop you from planting even the largest perennial in a container, but those that are very vigorous will need frequent repotting into larger containers; alternatively, you will have to divide the existing plant and repot it back into the same size pot. You will also have to water and feed them regularly or, once again, their stature will disappoint! The advantage of big plants in pots, however, is that you can move them around to do service in different ways: to screen a part of the garden you do not wish to have on view, to provide privacy or shelter, or a focal point for a seating area, for example.

The fact that containers can, with care, be moved around the garden is a useful attribute when you want to add sparkle to an area of the garden that lacks vertical interest. A patio looks flat and unappealing if its plants have no variations in height, but you can work wonders with just a few big perennials in pots. Some of the best for container growing are canna lilies.

Another bonus of planting big perennials in pots is that you can move them around to fill gaps in a border where a plant has failed to survive or thrive or is simply past its prime. You can also move pots closer to a seating area to take advantage of scented flowers: among those that are suitable for growing in pots are the richly perfumed lilies, like King lily (*Lilium regale*).

While the plants that do best in containers are those that prefer relatively dry conditions (in hot weather containers lose moisture at an alarming rate), if you are prepared to water your plants frequently and copiously, you can grow even moisture-loving plants in containers; however, be warned that in summer you will need to water them daily (or even several times a day) if they are to grow properly and achieve their "giant" proportions. Among good drought-resistant plants for pots are yuccas.

Make sure the containers you use have some aesthetic merit in their own right. Do not be tempted to economize. An imposing perennial demands an equally handsome pot in a good quality material—choose wood, stone, metal, or terra cotta, not plastic.

Pampas grass (Cortaderia selloana) *makes an unexpectedly dramatic feature when planted in large pots.*

Canna lilies are excellent candidates for pots, with their heavily veined leaves and brilliant spires of brightly colored flowers.

CULTIVATION AND MAINTENANCE

Getting started

You will need to look after your plants properly if they are going to reach their full potential. This section explains how to choose, plant, water, feed, and care for perennials, including advice on how to increase your stock and how to protect your plants from pests and diseases.

Buying plants

When it comes to stocking your garden, you can choose to buy your plants as container-grown specimens in nurseries or garden centers, by mail order (when they will be sent as bare-root plants), or you can grow them yourself from seeds or cuttings. Giant perennials are no different from other perennials in this respect, but for those unfamiliar with the basics of gardening, the following information is important.

Always take care when you buy plants that you purchase them from a good nursery or reputable garden center so that you can be sure they will get off to the best possible start. If you buy plants by mail order as bare-root plants,

BASIC TOOLS

remove the packaging and plunge the rootball into a bucket of water for 24 hours so that it can rehydrate properly before it is planted.

Basic equipment

If you are gardening for the first time, you will need to acquire a range of basic tools. The important ones are shown below, but whatever you buy, make sure they are of good quality and that you look after them well. The best ones are made of durable materials and are well balanced so that they are comfortable to use. You will be using them for a long time, so it pays to use the best. It also makes gardening more enjoyable.

Soil

To grow plants to the full height that nature intends, you need to provide them with the right conditons. The first of these is good garden soil or, at least, the soil that they prefer. Most plants do best in fertile garden soil to which good quantities of well-rotted compost have been added. This not only feeds the soil but also improves its structure. It helps to aerate heavy clay soil and, conversely, prevents light, sandy soil from draining too freely. If you are unsure about the composition of your soil, carry out a simple test. After rain, pick up a ball of soil in your hand and squeeze it; if it forms a sticky ball, your soil is a clay one. If it crumbles, you have normal loam. If it fails to form a ball and you can see gritty bits in it, it has a sandy base.

Soil pH

Most perennials grow best in soil that is neutral (with a pH value of around 6 to 7), but some plants prefer soil that is more or less acidic than the norm. If you do not know what your soil type is, take the trouble to do a simple pH test, which will indicate the levels of acidity or alkalinity. Because different areas of the same garden can have different pH levels, it is worth testing more than one area.

TESTING THE pH OF YOUR SOIL

A simple pH test will indicate levels of acidity/alkalinity in your soil. Kits can be bought from any garden center. Simply take a soil sample from your garden and add it to the test tube. The liquid will change color to indicate the pH, measured from 0–14. Low numbers indicate acidity; high numbers indicate alkalinity; neutral soil is around pH 7.

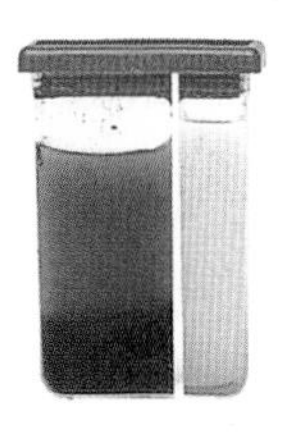

Acidic soil
Yellow or orange indicates that the soil is acidic.

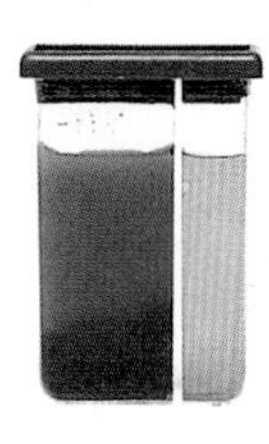

Neutral soil
Pale green indicates soil is neither acidic nor alkaline (neutral).

Alkaline soil
Dark green/ blue indicates that the soil is alkaline.

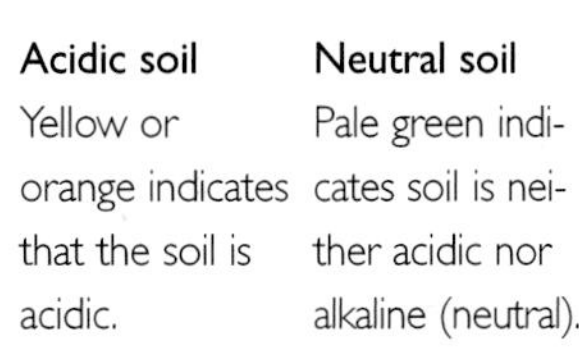

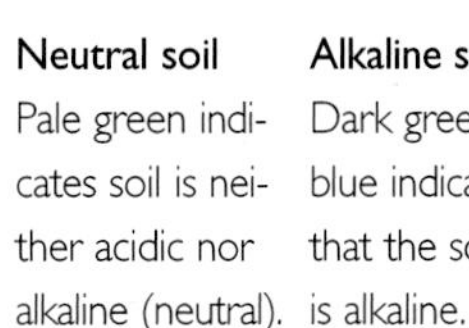

Planting your garden

Always dig a big enough hole for each new plant. It is tempting to skimp on this stage, but your plants will not thrive if their roots have to thrust their way through undug soil. Use a hand fork to loosen the soil in the bottom of the hole. Gently spread out the roots of the plant before planting (to make sure that they face outward and are not coiled around the rootball itself). Plants that have been kept for too long in a container will become pot-bound, when the leaves turn yellow and the plant eventually dies. Many plants that are container grown are part pot-bound, and the roots must be gently teased out.

Put a small handful of good-quality general fertilizer at the base of the planting hole (seaweed is a good organic choice that won't burn the roots), and make sure the crown of the plant is level with the surrounding soil. Backfill the planting hole, and firm the plant well. Add a stake if necessary and water in well. Finally, label the plant. This is more important than you might think, because in winter, when the leaves have disappeared, it is easy to forget what you put where or, if they are in containers, what the containers actually contain!

Climbers

If you are planting climbing plants, you will need to provide a secure support system for them. Normally this is done on either horizontal wires stretched along a supporting wall or by using a custom-made wooden trellis or wire mesh. When you plant the climber, support the leading stem with a stake to ensure that it grows upward vertically until it reaches the horizontal support system.

Once the main stem reaches the supports, the lateral shoots can be trained horizontally and will need to be tied in at intervals, using plastic plant ties or garden twine. Make sure that these are not so tight that they restrict growth or cut the plant. Training lateral shoots horizontally helps increase the number of flowering buds and improves the flowering quality of the plant.

HOW TO PLANT

Make sure that the planting hole is large enough to accommodate the root system. Firm plants in and water thoroughly.

RAISING A CLIMBER

1 Plant climbers at least 18in (45cm) from the wall so that the roots are not in a "rain shadow." Put a stake in the hole before adding the plant.

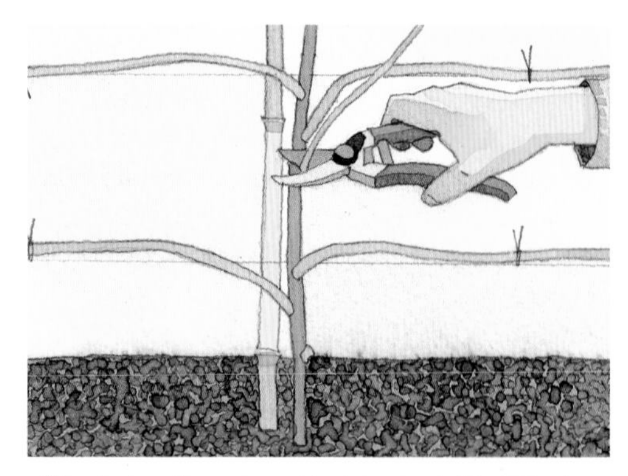

2 A clematis can be cut back to about 12in (30cm) from the ground after planting and at the end of the season. Tie in the stems as they develop.

WATERING SYSTEM

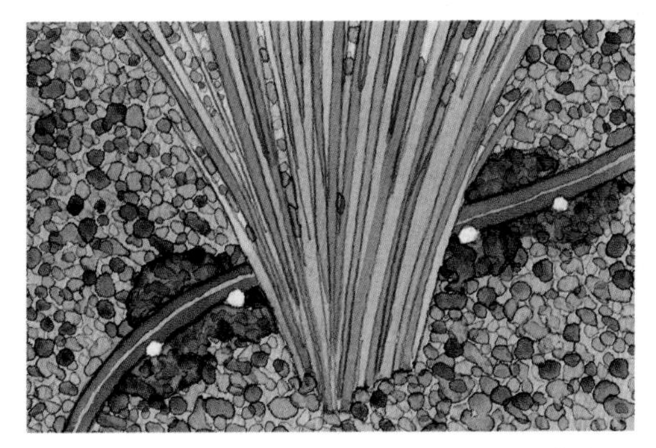

Some automatic watering systems involve laying garden hose with a series of holes in it around beds and borders.

Watering

No plant is going to survive unless it receives regular and appropriate amounts of water, and this is particularly true of plants that are expected to reach giant proportions. They do not necessarily need more water than smaller plants, but they need the quantities to which they have become adapted. Remember that winds have a desiccating (drying) effect, so sheltering tall plants by using screens as windbreaks can help to cut down moisture loss. Equally, mulching the soil surface with an inorganic or, better still, organic mulch will cut down moisture loss considerably, while having the added bonus that weeds will not grow as readily, being starved of essential light.

Watering always takes far longer than you think, but it is imperative that the water reaches right down to the roots, rather than simply wetting the leaves or the surface of the soil, so make sure you have plenty of time. If you water too little, you will end up with plants that develop shallow surface roots at the expense of deep roots, which makes them more prone to wilting when conditions become drier, thus exacerbating the problem.

You may find it helps to install a permanent irrigation system. There are various kinds available, ranging from simple "leaky" or drip hose systems, which are lengths of garden hose punctured with small holes, to more sophisticated systems, with sensors that detect the level of moisture in the soil and switch on automatically when moisture levels are low. These have branching systems that allow you to direct the water exactly where it is needed, but the fine nozzles can become clogged. You should explore the options carefully and seek advice from your local garden center or gardening club, because some of the more sophisticated systems are expensive.

Feeding

In the past, gardeners had their own favorite recipes for preparations made from the basic nutrients and minerals available. These days, most people prefer to buy their fertilizers already mixed. The multipurpose fertilizers that are widely available have been formulated with a balance of nutrients and minerals, of which the three major ones are nitrogen (N), phosphorus (P), and potassium (K), along with secondary nutrients, such as sulfur, magnesium, and calcium, and minerals such as boron, magnesium, and zinc. One of the best multipurpose plant foods is seaweed-based fertilizer, which includes all the major and minor nutrients that plants need. Compost is also a rich source of nutrients.

The aim is to get the nutrients to the roots of the plants, so you need to fertilize the soil in which the plants will be grown. Additional fertilizers that are needed at certain times of the year—during flower formation, for example—can be applied directly to the leaves, where the uptake will be more immediate. Foliar feeds are therefore generally regarded as a quick pick-me-up for plants. Generally, however, perennials do not need elaborate feeding, as long as the soil is in good condition and compost applied regularly.

FEEDING

In early spring apply a handful of a slow-release fertilizer around the base of each plant, forking it in lightly and watering after feeding. Make sure that the fertilizer does not actually touch the plant, as it may scorch it.

Routine care

In an established garden, most plants will need little more than routine care in summer to keep them looking their best. If you keep on top of these tasks, gardening will always be a pleasure and never a burden.

Weeding

To keep your plants healthy, you must remove any competition from weeds. To prevent weeds from becoming established in the first place, mulch your borders and beds whenever you can, as this will cut down on the work. When you create a new bed, you must remove all traces of perennial weeds; otherwise, they will simply resprout, usually in even greater numbers. Chopping through the roots of couch grass, for example, simply increases the number of eventual grass plants that will arise. Throw out all perennial weeds (do not compost them). Among those commonly found in gardens are couch grass, ground elder, dock, bindweed, plantain, and sorrel.

Keep your borders weeded regularly, so that weeds do not seed themselves and proliferate even more. Annual weeds can be removed easily with a hoe; perennial weeds with a taproot will have to be removed individually with a hand fork or try pulling them with the soil wet.

If you don't want your chosen perennials to self-seed, remove the flowerheads before seeds form; otherwise, some will self-sow so enthusiastically that they become "weeds."

Mulching

To help slow down water evaporation and to prevent weeds from growing, it pays to mulch your plants well. There is a range of mulches available, and it makes good organic sense to use those that are available locally. They can vary from bark chips and cocoa shells to mussel shells, gravel, and straw. Organic mulches have the bonus that they will provide nutrients as well as protection, but inorganic ones need less frequent renewal.

MULCH	REPLACE	PROS AND CONS
Straw	Replace annually	Organic; messy; inexpensive
Bark chips	Renew every 2 years	Organic; fairly durable; aesthetically pleasing; provides no nutrients; expensive
Well-rotted compost	Renew annually	Organic; improves soil fertility; improves water retention; free
Gravel	Renew every 3–4 years	Inorganic; good weed suppressant; provides no nutrients; expensive
Black plastic	Renew every 3–4 years	Inorganic; good weed suppressant; provides no nutrients; relatively inexpensive.

WEEDING

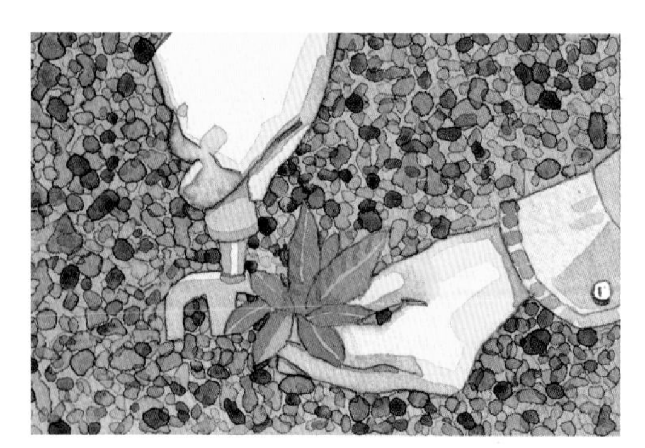

Perennial weeds need to be dug out and burned. Use a hand fork to prize the roots from the soil. If you weed after it has rained, the ground is easier to work. Burn perennial weeds.

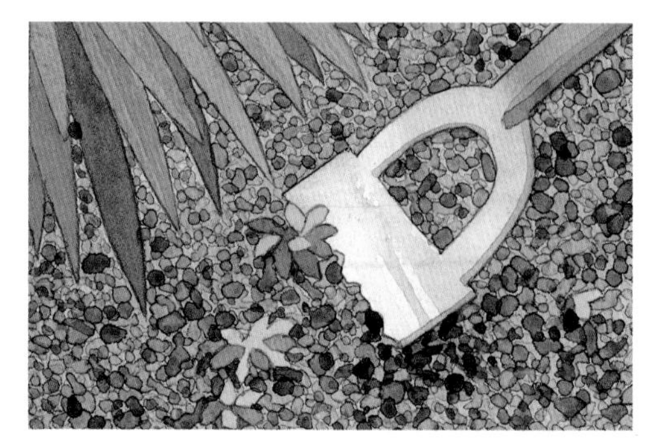

A hoe can be used to remove weed seedlings. Depending on the style of hoe, you can draw it along the surface of the soil or use a light chopping motion. Annual weeds can be composted.

If you cover the crown of a slightly tender plant in winter with a mulch, you may nurse it through colder spells.

Staking

Soft-stemmed perennials will require staking to keep them upright; this is particularly true of the giant perennials—because of their height, they are more vulnerable to wind damage. Which plants require staking and which do not depends to some degree on local climate as well as the plant's actual growth habit, but providing some kind of shelter will minimize the damage.

The aim of staking is to keep it discreet. You want to look at the plant, not the stake. There is a wide range of custom-made stakes available, of which the best are those that can be adapted to suit the height and habit of the plants. Linked stakes are popular, as you put the individual components together to make the stake of the width you require.

One of the simplest and most effective staking systems for clump-forming perennials is to use brushwood sticks inserted around the plant. These are almost invisible to the eye but do the job efficiently, so if you have prunings of suitably twiggy shrubs, keep them for this purpose. For single-stemmed perennials, such as delphiniums, a single bamboo or plastic cane, tied at intervals with a loose plastic tie, is the most commonly used device. For clumps of plants, you can set four canes around the plant, spacing them evenly, and tie these together with string to make an encircling frame for the plant's stems. Beware, however, that the tips of these canes can be dangerous—when you bend to weed it is only too easy to damage your eyes, so give each cane a protective rubber stopper or similar safety device.

Deadheading

Removing spent flowers (known as deadheading) is done for several reasons. First, from an aesthetic point of view, flowers that have large, striking blooms are particularly noticeable when the flowers die and fade, so removing them helps to ensure that the remaining display is not spoiled. Second, deadheading encourages more flower buds to form, extending the flowering season. Finally, removing spent flowers from plants that self-seed vigorously helps to keep them under control. However, it would be a mistake to think that all fading flowerheads should be removed; in many plants, the seedheads that follow are one of the attractions in the final months of the year.

Overwintering plants

Contrary to popular belief, it is not just extremely low temperatures that kills plants—it is the condition of the plants when the frosts strike that is most likely to do the damage. Plants that are still full of sap when an unexpectedly cold spell occurs are more likely to succumb than those that are not, and a cold spell immediately following a wet spell will kill more plants than would otherwise fall victim. Avoid feeding plants once autumn starts. Make sure that the beds and borders drain well, because waterlogging coupled with freezing conditions will kill many plants that might otherwise survive. Those plants that are debatably hardy in your area can sometimes be nursed through the winter with a mulch over the crown of the plant, which acts rather like a blanket does. Do not be tempted to remove this winter "blanket" too soon. Spring can be a treacherously changeable season.

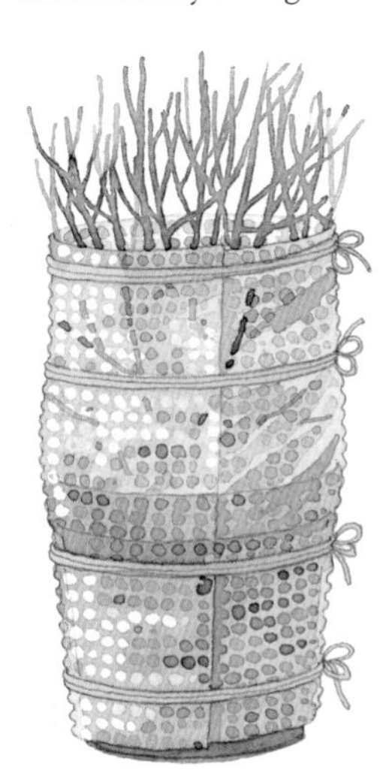

Containers can be bubble-wrapped or covered in burlap to provide extra protection, or, indeed, moved indoors in freezing weather.

Propagation

Buying new plants is an expensive business, and it is usually worth increasing your stock of plants by propagating them yourself. There are two main ways of doing this. One is by sowing seed; the other is by persuading other parts of the plant (stems, leaves, or roots) to grow roots to become a new plant. You can also propagate plants by simply dividing up the existing clumps, taking care that each new clump sports at least one healthy growing shoot. The individual entries in the Plant Directory suggest the ways in which you can propagate your stock.

Sowing seed

Growing from seed is generally easy and inexpensive, but it takes longer than it will from cuttings. The seed packets you purchase invariably give you all the information you require about the best time to sow, the depth to sow, and so forth.

You need to sow in fine compost that is specially formulated for seeds. You must make sure that the seeds and seedlings receive adequate amounts of light and moisture, and that the temperature is suitable and constant. You can sow seeds in a wide variety of containers, from small seed flats to individual plastic pots. Your choice will depend on the habit of the plant and how easily it transplants to its permanent home. Many perennials can be sown *in situ*, in the ground, but you must remember that you have done so, and do not dig them up by mistake or weed them out!

Sowing seeds in rows, rather than distributing the seeds at random, helps you to remove the plants when you need to transplant them. If you sow the seeds using a piece of folded card to distribute the seeds, it will be easier to make sure that they are evenly spaced. Make sure you label all sown seeds immediately. It is surprisingly easy to forget what you have only recently sown. Write the sowing date on the label as well, and then cover the tray or pot with plastic wrap or a sheet of glass to maintain even warmth and humidity.

Once the seedlings have developed two true leaves, as opposed to their first seedling leaves, they can be potted up or transplanted into their permanent places. Seed sown in early spring indoors will need to be acclimatized to outdoor conditions gradually (hardening off), usually by putting the tray outside for several hours in the daytime and bringing it in at night over several days.

Taking cuttings

Success with cuttings is not guaranteed. Some plants take more easily than others, but it is always worth a try, since it takes relatively little time to do. Stem cuttings tend to root most easily, and the best time to take them is when the plant is putting out new growth (but is not actually in flower or about to flower), or again when flowering has ceased and new leafy growth is made in early autumn. Not all plants can be

SOWING SEED

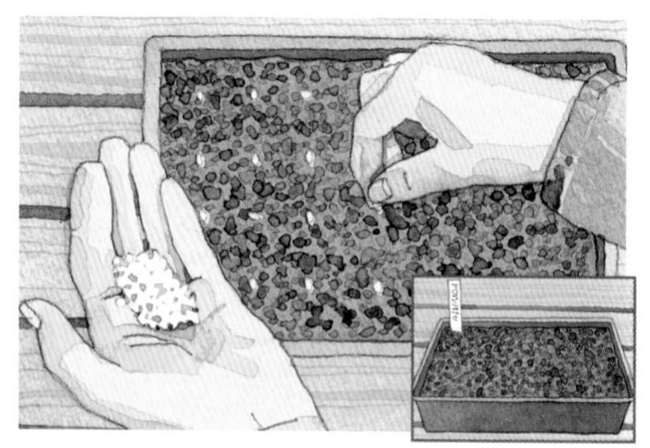

1 Fill a seed tray with compost that is formulated for seeds. Do not use garden soil. Space the seeds evenly over the surface, cover with a fine layer of sifted compost, and water carefully. Add a label.

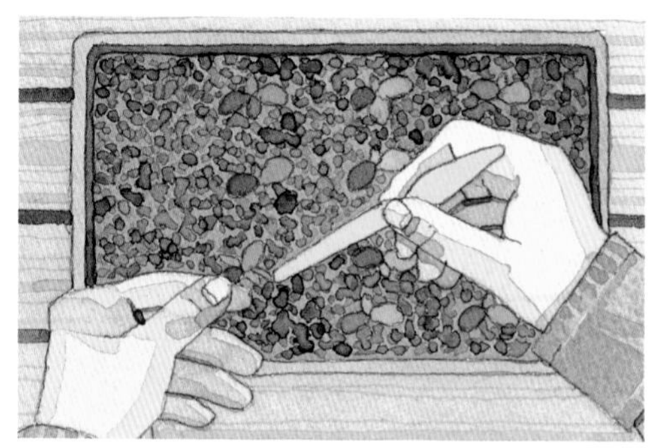

2 When the seedlings have developed their first true leaves, carefully pot them into individual small containers, making sure you do not touch the stems which bruise easily. Water them well after transplanting.

TAKING STEM CUTTINGS

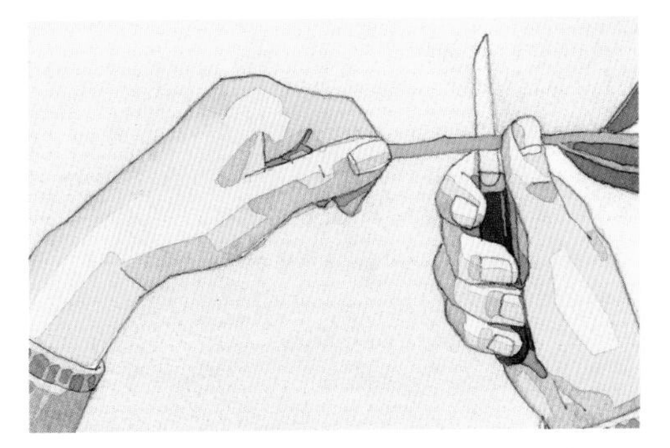

1 Remove the cutting from the parent plant, taking a new shoot about 3in (8cm) long. Remove the bottom leaves but take care that you do not tear the plant tissue.

2 Into the cuttings compost (formulated to be fairly free-draining) insert the cuttings about 1in (2.5cm) deep. Label the cuttings. Water well and cover with a plastic bag or put them in a propagator.

propagated from cuttings; some cuttings may rot before new roots form.

Cuttings should be taken only from healthy plants, and you should make sure that at least one leaf node (the bump where the leaf starts) is buried in the compost with the base of the cutting, as this is where the new roots will form.

A few leaves are removed from the bottom of cuttings, so that they do not waste too much energy on existing leaf growth; the energy needs to go into creating roots on the base section of the cutting.

Root cuttings

Plants with fleshy roots, such as Japanese anemones, leopard plants, and coneflowers, often take well from root cuttings. Root cuttings are taken in early autumn, and the biggest single problem is making sure that you plant the root cuttings with the right end up. Dig up the plant from which the cuttings are to be taken, and then cut sections of root; using a sharp, sterile garden knife make a slanting cut at the base of the root and a horizontal one at the top. When you have laid out the cuttings and are ready to plant them, you will know which end is which. Replant the parent plant before the rootball dies out.

Dividing perennials

Many perennials are clump-forming and require dividing to ensure that they maintain their health and vigor. The center will eventually die out as the new roots and growth spread outward, which is another good reason for division. The new divisions can be used to form new plants, so this is a useful system of propagation for many plants.

TAKING ROOT CUTTINGS

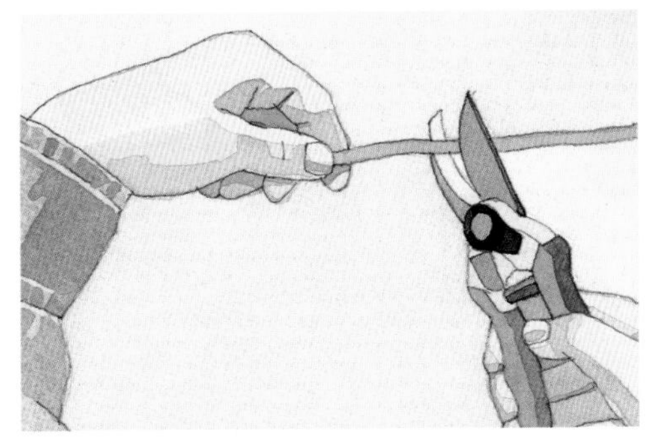

1 Carefully wash the soil away from the roots and cut off one or more roots. Cut the root into pieces no more than 3in (8cm) long, making a differently angled cut at top and bottom, so you can tell which way up to plant them.

2 Insert the cuttings into good-quality compost with the base of the cutting (the cut from the furthest section of root away from the crown) downmost. Water and place in a plastic bag or propagator.

Pests and diseases

The best way to prevent and control the ravages of pests and diseases is to ensure that your plants are in tip-top condition and aren't unnecessarily stressed. Inadequate and infrequent watering and feeding will add to stress, making plants prone to viral diseases in particular. If you keep an eye on your plants, you can usually prevent any incipient attacks by pests before they take hold. Plant breeding now makes it possible to buy virus-resistant cultivars of many plants. Another way to prevent diseases from building up is to allow as much air circulation as possible.

Lack of trace elements in the soil can be a serious problem; if your plants look unexpectedly sickly, test the soil's condition. Kits are available in the garden centers, or you can get the soil tested by professional organizations.

Organic versus chemical approach

Most people prefer to follow an organic approach to pest and disease control, although even those who would rather be organic may resort to chemicals when a major problem threatens. Remember that even some of the organically acceptable pesticides, such as pyrethrin and rotenone, are toxic, and you should take the usual precautions (goggles, gloves etc.) when using them.

Controlling Giant Perennials

Some plants are banned in certain American states and Canadian provinces, where they are known as "noxious plants" as they can grow out of control. See page 143 for more information about this.

COMMON DISEASES

DISEASE	SYMPTOMS	REMEDY
Botrytis/Grey mold Serious secondary infection, often following untreated mildews	Discolored, yellowing leaves eventually covered with grayish felt	*Remove affected parts and burn them. Spray with carbendazim* HOW TO AVOID *Improve air circulation around plants*
Downy mildew	Discolored yellowing leaves with grayish-white patches on undersides	*Remove affected parts and burn. Spray with mancozeb* HOW TO AVOID *Improve air circulation around plants. Avoid overhead watering*
Powdery mildew Caused by various fungi that thrive in plants grown on dry soil	Floury white patches on leaves, distorted shoots, premature leaf fall	*Prune out affected parts. Spray with fungicide, such as bupirimate or sulfur* HOW TO AVOID *Improve air circulation around plants*
Root rot	Top parts of plants wilt and die as roots rot	*Remove plant* HOW TO AVOID *Improve drainage by adding grit to soil to prevent waterlogging*
Verticillium wilt Fungus causing damage to stems and roots	Vertical brown stripes on stems so that plants deteriorate	*Remove plants and affected soil in the vicinity* HOW TO AVOID *Keep weeds under control and clean pruning tools regularly*

COMMON PESTS

PEST	SYMPTOMS	CONTROL
Aphids Dense colonies of small, pale green, pink, or greenish-black, sap-sucking insects	Distorted leaves and shoots; sticky coating on leaves, sometimes with sooty mold	*Check plants frequently and remove small colonies by hand; encourage natural predators (birds, ladybugs, lacewings, earwigs); spray with malathion or pirimicarb*
Earwigs Dark brown insects with pincers at rear	Small, circular holes or notches in leaves or flowers	*Trap insects in straw-filled pots supported on canes; spray or dust with malathion (only if damage is serious)*
Leaf miners Small insect larvae feed on the leaves	White or pale green blotches or tracks on foliage	*Remove damaged leaves; spray with malathion or pirimiphos-methyl*
Scale insects Small brown sap-sucking insects, resembling tiny blisters, on stems and undersides of leaves	Stunted growth of leaves; yellowing leaves; sooty black mold	*Spray with malathion*
Slugs and snails Crawling pests that leave a slimy trail	Circular holes in plant tissue; young plants may be completely destroyed	*Apply slug pellets; use slug traps filled with beer; encourage natural predators (birds, hedgehogs); apply nematodes (which parasitize slugs and snails)*
Vine weevils Dark brown insects and white, C-shaped grubs	The insects eat notches out of leaves; the soil-dwelling larvae eat roots, sometimes causing plants to collapse altogether	*Apply parasitic nematodes to warm soil to kill the larvae; apply pirimiphos-methyl; use non-drying glue around containers to prevent adults from reaching the soil to lay eggs*
Wireworms Thin, yellow, worm-like bodies, pointed at each end	Holes in roots and tubers	*Apply pirimiphos-methyl as dust or granules at planting*

PLANT DIRECTORY

Achillea

ASTERACEAE/COMPOSITAE

Yarrow

The genus *Achillea* contains some 115 species of herbaceous perennials from temperate zones throughout the Northern Hemisphere. Those that grow naturally on grassland tend to be much bigger than those that grow in mountainous areas, but they are all characterized by deep green, ferny foliage (which is sometimes aromatic) and clusters of daisylike, white, pink or yellow flowers that are borne in large, flat heads and last from summer to fall. Yarrows are worth growing to use as cut flowers, and they also dry well.

Most yarrows generally reach about 3ft (1m) in height. However, cultivars of fernleaf yarrow (*Achillea filipendulina*), such as 'Cloth of Gold', which has deep golden flowers and light green leaves, will grow to 5ft (1.5m) tall. *A. f.* 'Coronation Gold', also with golden-yellow flowers but gray-green foliage, will grow to 3ft (90cm).

WHERE TO PLANT

Yarrows do best in moist soil, but they need good drainage and full sun for best performance. On the whole, however, they are not particularly fussy and will tolerate partial shade and drier conditions.

PLANT CARE

Sow seeds *in situ* in late summer or divide existing clumps in spring. The sturdy stems can be cut back in late autumn or left until spring. The most common problem affecting yarrows is powdery mildew, although aphid attacks can also occur.

PLANTING SUGGESTIONS

These are excellent plants for a mixed border, where they provide structure for lower-growing plants. The slightly smaller 'Credo', which has lemony yellow flowers, makes a good companion for the taller forms.

Achilleas are excellent border plants, bearing many showy flattish flowerheads.

A. filipendulina *is a relative giant, and therefore good for the back of the border, with its glistening heads of golden yellow flowers (above and left).*

Aconitum

RANUNCULACEAE

Monkshood, Aconite

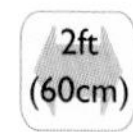

This large genus from the Northern Hemisphere contains perennials, biennials, and even a couple of climbers, and it has a long history in cultivation. All parts of the plant are poisonous, and the foliage can cause blisters on sensitive skin. The flowers stand above the leaves in elegant spires. The foliage is deeply divided and is a dark, rich green.

Plants sold as Carmichael's monkshood (*Aconitum carmichaelii* Wilsonii Group) are late-flowering (late summer to early autumn) and have dusky purple-blue flowers in spires that grow to 6ft (1.8m). *A.* x *cammarum* 'Stainless Steel', a recent introduction, has slate blue flowers in midsummer and in the right conditions reaches 5ft (1.5m). The older cultivar *A.* 'Spark's Variety' also grows to 5ft (1.5m) in the right position; it is worth planting for its deep indigo blue flowers, which are carried in branching spires. Wolfsbane (*A. lycoctonum*) has similarly shaped flowers, but they are yellow not purple. Several cultivars developed from Venus's chariot, also called Turk's-cap, (*A. napellus*) reach good heights, including *A. n.* 'Newry Blue', which has mid-blue flowers.

WHERE TO PLANT

Monkshoods do best in moist soil and partial shade, where they will reach their greatest heights; however, they will also cope with full sun.

PLANT CARE

Sow seeds in late spring. Divide established plants every year in early autumn. The tallest forms will need staking. Cut plants to ground level in autumn and apply a mulch. Fungal stem rot can be a problem, and plants can be damaged by aphids. Verticillium wilt can, over a couple of years, destroy plants.

PLANTING SUGGESTIONS

Plant monkshoods where their flowering spires can be shown off at the back of a mixed border.

Aconitum *'Spark's Variety' is a well-known cultivar with deep blue flowers.*

Alcea

MALVACEAE

Hollyhock

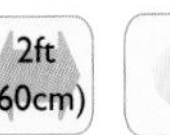

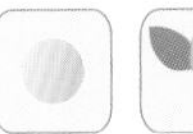

This genus of short-lived perennials and biennials, thought to have originated in Asia, is found in the temperate zones of Asia and Europe. It includes the popular garden hollyhock (*Alcea rosea*), a biennial, which reaches 8ft (2.5m) in the right conditions and spreads to about 2ft (60cm). The leaves are light green and slightly hairy, with five or seven lobes and conspicuous veins. The flowers, which can be up to 3in (8cm) across, have five petals and are funnel-shaped and borne in tall spires. The flowers of the species are single and white or shades of purple, pink, or yellow. There are many good cultivars, most of which have large, double flowers in a wide range of colors. *A. rosea* Chater's Double Group has double flowers in a vast color range; 'Indian Spring' has single flowers, also in many colors; and 'Nigra' has rich chocolate brown single flowers with a noticeable yellow throat.

WHERE TO PLANT

Hollyhocks prefer fairly rich, well-drained soil and a sheltered position in full sun. Plants grown on exposed, windy sites will require staking.

PLANT CARE

Sow seeds in warmth in early spring or *in situ* in late spring. They will flower the year after being sown, and you can transplant them, if necessary, once they have acquired their "true" leaves. If you grow new hollyhocks every year from seed, you will eliminate the likelihood of rust (identified by small, orange-brown spores on stems and leaves), which can be a major problem when hollyhocks are grown as perennials. Young hollyhocks may be attacked by slugs, snails, and cutworms. Aphids and mirid (capsid) bugs can also cause problems.

PLANTING SUGGESTIONS

Hollyhocks are often grown in mixed borders—but look just as good against a sunny wall.

The hollyhock's (Alcea) dramatic spires of saucer-shaped flowers make an eye-catching display in the summer.

Allium

ALLIACEAE

Onion

Of the 690 or so species in this vast genus of bulbous and rhizomatous perennials, only two qualify for the epithet "giant"—*Allium giganteum* and *A. stipitatum*. The aptly named *A. giganteum* is the most commonly cultivated. It grows from a bulb and has broad, strap-shaped, mid-green leaves that are over 3ft (90cm) long. These normally wither away before the flowers appear in the summer. The flowers are dense, ball-shaped heads up to 4in (10cm) in diameter and composed of more than 50 tiny, star-shaped, lilac pink flowers with noticeable stamens. The flowers are borne on upright stems that reach up to 6ft (1.8m) in height. *A. stipitatum* (zones 4–10) grows to only 5ft (1.5m). It has shorter, gray-green leaves but similarly large heads of pale lilac flowers in summer.

WHERE TO PLANT

All onions prefer fertile, well-drained soil and a sunny site, although they will grow adequately in light shade.

PLANT CARE

The bulbs should be planted about 3in (8cm) deep (or twice the depth of the bulb) in autumn. A little sand at the bottom of the planting hole will improve drainage. Propagate bulbous alliums by removing offsets from around the bulbs in autumn and planting them; however, as long as the bulbs are flowering well, they should be left undisturbed. Although generally easy to grow, alliums can suffer from white rot, downy mildew and onion fly.

PLANTING SUGGESTIONS

Grow smaller alliums alongside the taller species: Stars-of-Persia (*A. Cristophii*) (zones 4–10), for example, which grows to about 3ft (90cm), has large, delicate heads of metallic purple flowers; and daffodil garlic (*A. neapolitanum*) grows 16in (40cm) high and bears clusters of pure white, star-shaped flowers. The flowerheads dry well and are often used in dried flower arrangements.

Although not truly a giant, A. cristophii *will look good with other taller alliums.*

Anemone

RANUNCULACEAE

Windflower

This large genus, known as windflowers or lilies-of-the-field, contains about 140 species. Some species are tiny, and Japanese anemone (*Anemone* x *hybrida*, a cross between *A. hupehensis* var. *japonica* and *A. vitifolia*) is the only member of this genus that can truly be considered "giant." It is an herbaceous perennial with suckering shoots. The mid-green, hand-shaped leaves are toothed and have three lobes; the leaves at the base of the plant are larger than those further up the stem. The flowers of *A.* x *hybrida* are semi-double and white or pale pink, about 3in (8cm) across, and are borne over a long season from midsummer to mid-autumn.

There are several good cultivars to look out for. 'White Giant' and 'White Queen' have semi-double, white flowers. 'Honorine Jobert' (sometimes sold as *A.* x *hybrida* 'Alba') also has white flowers, with prominent yellow stamens. 'Queen Charlotte' has semi-double, silver-pink flowers. The strongly growing 'Profusion' has large, pink, semi-double flowers to 3in (8cm) across.

WHERE TO PLANT

These vigorous plants are good subjects for lightly shaded or east- or north-facing borders. They prefer moisture-retentive, humus-rich soil but will not tolerate waterlogged conditions.

PLANT CARE

Plants can be propagated from seed in late summer (scrape the outer coating of the seed first to encourage germination). Divide established clumps after three years in early spring or autumn. Mulch the crowns in winter in cold areas. Although susceptible to eelworm, leaf spot, powdery mildew, and slug and snail attacks, they tend to be fairly trouble-free.

PLANTING SUGGESTIONS

Japanese anemones are ideal beneath deciduous trees, where the clumps will increase in size if left undisturbed. They are useful in mixed borders, as they flower from late summer to autumn.

In the right conditions, Anemone *'Honorine Jobert' will spread to form large clumps.*

Angelica archangelica

APIACEAE/UMBELLIFERAE

Angelica, Wild parsnip

The plants in the genus *Angelica* are biennials or fairly short-lived herbaceous perennials, and are found in damp woodlands and meadows in many parts of the Northern Hemisphere. The most frequently seen and planted species is Angelica (*Angelica archangelica*), an herb with both culinary and medicinal uses, and a really striking plant. From early- to midsummer, it bears huge heads, which can be 10in (25cm) across, of greenish-yellow flowers on thick, ribbed stems. The leaves are toothed and lance-shaped.

Woodland angelica (*A. sylvestris*) (zones 3–9) can be even bigger—up to 6½ft (2m) tall. A short-lived perennial or biennial, it is late-flowering—from midsummer to fall—with white or pink flowers. The leaves are large (up to 2ft (60cm) long) and the stems are flushed pinkish-purple.

WHERE TO PLANT

Plant angelica in fertile, moist soil in sun or partial shade. *A. sylvestris* prefers full sun.

PLANT CARE

These robust, upright plants should not normally require staking. If you deadhead angelica before it goes to seed, it will flower in the second year. You can propagate plants from seeds as soon as they are ripe, but the seeds will not germinate unless they are exposed to light. Seedlings resent handling once they are large, so plant them out into their permanent positions while they are still small. They are prone to slug and snail damage, and, if the summer is dry, they are susceptible to powdery mildew.

PLANTING SUGGESTIONS

Plant Angelica in the back of a border or in an herb garden. Woodland angelica is better suited to a wild or woodland garden.

The large, delicate umbels of Angelica flowers catch the light beautifully.

Aralia

ARALIACEAE

Aralia

The genus *Aralia* includes over 30 species of evergreen and deciduous trees and shrubs, as well as the rhizomatous perennials described here, which are native to North America and are found in the wild growing in mountainous woodlands.

Elk clover (*Aralia californica*) bursts into growth in spring and puts on a rapid 6–7ft (1.8–2.2m) by late summer. The divided leaves are shallowly toothed. The plant bears large clusters of greenish-white flowers in summer, followed by small black berries in autumn.

American spikenard (*A. racemosa*) (zones 5–9) grows to an even more impressive 10ft (3m) and has a widely spreading habit, to 4ft (1.2m) across. The leaves are mid-green and divided, and each leaf may be 30in (75cm) long. In summer, Spikenard bears large clusters of greenish-white flowers in spikes that grow up to 16in (40cm) long; the flowers are followed by clusters of small, purplish berries in autumn.

WHERE TO PLANT

Grow these rhizomatous aralias in humus-rich, reliably moist soil. They will cope with partial shade but need protection from strong winds.

PLANT CARE

Cut back plants to the ground in autumn, after fruiting, and apply a mulch around the crowns. Propagate in spring from seed (scrape the outer casing to improve germination). Alternatively, propagate from root cuttings in winter. Divide established clumps every two to three years. They are generally trouble-free, but aphids sometimes attack young shoots in early summer.

PLANTING SUGGESTIONS

These potentially large plants need careful siting because they grow so large so quickly. In a sheltered garden, they are excellent plants for the poolside or for the edge of a woodland area.

*Spikenard (*Aralia racemosa*) is one of the most impressive giant perennials. However, they are not ideal for a small, mixed border, where they will overpower daintier neighbours.*

Artemisia

ASTERACEAE/COMPOSITAE

Sagebrush, Mugwort, Wormwood

This is a large genus of perennials, annuals and evergreen and deciduous shrubs that originated from drier areas in the Northern Hemisphere (although some are found in South Africa and South America). Of the available species, one can be called "giant." White mugwort (*Artemisia lactiflora*), a clump-forming perennial, has deeply dissected, dark green leaves and bears airy clusters of white flowers for a long season from midsummer to mid-autumn. Plants reach 5ft (1.5m) high with a spread of 2ft (60cm).

There are a few interesting cultivars, including plants sold as Guizhou Group (syn. *A. lactiflora* var. *purpurea*), which are more stiffly erect than the species and have purplish young foliage, and *A. l.* 'Jim Russell', which has a more arching habit. The German cultivar *A.* 'Rosenschleier' grows up to 5ft (1.5m) tall and has clusters of dusky pink flowers in late summer to mid-autumn. All of these plants are excellent as cut flowers.

WHERE TO PLANT

Grow in moisture-retentive but well-drained soil in full sun. Most artemisias do best in fairly dry soil, but the plants discussed need reliably moist conditions.

PLANT CARE

These plants do not need staking. Cut them back to the base in late autumn, when the flowers have faded. You can propagate from seed sown in spring or autumn or from greenwood cuttings or heel cuttings taken in summer. Divide established clumps every couple of years. Sagebrush are generally trouble-free, but white mugwort is prone to powdery mildew if the weather is dry for long periods.

PLANTING SUGGESTIONS

The slightly smaller western mugwort (*A. ludoviciana* 'Silver Queen'), which grows to about 4ft (1.2m), has long, lance-shaped, silver-white leaves and contrasts well in a mixed border.

*The delicate flowers and divided leaves of white mugwort (*Artemisia lactiflora*) produce an ethereal effect.*

Arruncus dioicus

ROSACEAE

Goatsbeard

This clump-forming perennial is found in moist woodland areas in the mountainous regions of the Northern Hemisphere, and it looks much like both meadowsweet (*Filipendula*) and spiraea (*Spiraea*) (with which it used to be grouped botanically). It has mid-green, fernlike leaves, about 3ft (1m) long, and the flowers are borne in loose, pyramid-shaped spires from mid-spring to midsummer.

The flowers of female plants are pendant and greenish-white; those of male plants are more erect and more creamy in color. It will make a handsome clump about 6ft (1.8m) tall and 4ft (1.2m) wide.

WHERE TO PLANT

Goatsbeard grows best in moist conditions and is a good choice for a site near water or in a specially constructed bog garden. It isn't particularly fussy about soil type but prefers shade or partial shade. Although it will tolerate drier conditions and a position in full sun, it will not do as well.

PLANT CARE

Seed can be sown in autumn or spring, but plants will self-seed freely unless deadheaded, so you do not need to sow seed to propagate it. Divide established clumps every two or three years in fall or spring. It is not troubled by much, but blackfly and sawfly larvae may possibly cause problems.

PLANTING SUGGESTIONS

Grow at the back of a large mixed border in a shady area. The widely grown cultivar *A. dioicus* 'Kneiffii' is smaller, growing about 4ft (1.2m) high and 18in (45cm) across, and has small, arching, cream flowers and more deeply divided leaves; it is a better choice for a small bed.

*Goatsbeard (*Aruncus dioicus*) is a good choice for damp gardens, especially in shaded borders.*

Aster

ASTERACEAE/COMPOSITAE

Michaelmas daisy, Aster

This diverse genus of more than 250 species contains annuals and subshrubs, as well as the familiar perennials and biennials. They feature daisylike flowers composed of numerous long, narrow petals arranged around a central eye. The colors range from white to deepest purple, via blues, mauves and pinks. The leaves are generally simple, lance-shaped and mid-green.

While some asters are tiny enough for a rock garden, there are some species and cultivars that deserve the epithet "giant." These include *Aster umbellatus*, a species aster that is best suited to wilder parts of the garden. It rises to 7ft (2.2m) and has small white flowers with yellow eyes. There are a number of tall cultivars of blue wood aster (*A. cordifolius*), an aster with loose clusters of light to deep blue flowers from late summer to mid-autumn. Among them are 'Chieftain', which grows to 6ft (1.8m) tall and bears tiny, pale lilac flowers. 'Climax', a mildew-resistant hybrid, has large purple flowers and grows to 5ft (1.5m). New England aster (*A. novae-angliae*) is another big aster, growing to 5ft (1.5m) tall, with sprays of violet-purple flowers from late summer to mid-autumn. Among the cultivars to look out for are the lilac-pink 'Lye End Beauty', which grows over 5ft (1.5m) tall; the deep pink 'Andenken an Alma Pötschke', which grows to about 5ft (1.5m); and 'Barr's Violet', which also grows to about 5ft (1.5m) tall, but with deep violet-blue flowers.

WHERE TO PLANT

Planting position will depend on the species or group to which the asters belong. Blue wood aster and its cultivars and *A. umbellatus* will grow in partial shade in moderately fertile soil. New England aster and its cultivars prefer well-cultivated, fertile, reliably moist soil and will cope with sun or partial shade.

Asters look good when planted with later-flowering grasses. There is a good range of cultivars in shades from pinkish mauve (shown here, above and left) to violet blue.

PLANT CARE

Asters tend to flop, so stake them with inconspicuous stakes. Cut back asters in late autumn after flowering, after which they should be mulched. Alternatively, replant every year incorporating plenty of humus into the soil. You can replant asters from divided clumps or from runners, or you can sow seed in spring or autumn. Asters can be troubled by a range of problems, the most common being mildew, and it is always worth looking out for mildew-resistant cultivars, of which increasing numbers are becoming available. Fusarium wilt and leaf spot are also common problems. Of the pests, eelworms, aphids, slugs and snails will attack asters, but the most important pest is tarsonemid mite which prevents *A. novi-belgii*—and maybe some other species—from producing flowers.

PLANTING SUGGESTIONS

Because they have small flowers, asters look best planted in large drifts, which also helps to minimize any flopping. They look good with other daisylike plants, such as sneezeweed (*Helenium*) and with late-flowering grasses.

*The New England Aster (*A. novae-angliae*) is one of the largest asters, creating a long-lasting display of pinkish mauve flowers from late summer to the middle of autumn.*

Astilbe

SAXIFRAGACEAE

Astilbe

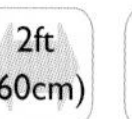

Originating in Southeast Asia and North America, this genus of some 14 species of rhizomatous perennials grows naturally in moist woodlands. Closely resembling smaller versions of goatsbeard (*Aruncus dioicus*), astilbes produce eye-catching plumes of flowers in white and shades of red, pink and purple, as well as elegant leaves that grow up to 2ft (60cm) long and are divided into leaflets.

Astilbes have been the subject of fairly intensive breeding, which has resulted in some large hybrids and cultivars. Of the species, two from China are significantly large: *Astilbe grandis* grows to 5ft (1.5m) and has plumes of white flowers in summer; *A. rivularis* grows even larger, to 6ft (1.8m) tall, and also has white flowers but with magnificent leaves that make a large basal clump.

There are many hybrids available. *A.* 'Professor van der Wielen' grows to 4ft (1.2m), and *A.* 'Jo Ophorst' grows to 4½ft (1.4m).

WHERE TO PLANT

Astilbes need fertile soil and will not survive in soils that dry out quickly. Give them plenty of humus in a rich, moist site in sun.

PLANT CARE

Divide clumps every few years to maintain vigor. Propagate by division. Astilbes are generally trouble-free, but powdery mildew and leaf spot can occur.

PLANTING SUGGESTIONS

Astilbes make good bog-side plants.

Astilbes do best in fertile soil, producing drifts of plume-like flowers.

Baptisia

LEGUMINOSAE/PAPILIONACEAE

False indigo, Wild indigo

This genus of about 30–35 herbaceous perennials originates in North America, where they are found in grasslands or dry woodlands. Blue false indigo (*Baptisia australis*), the most widely grown species, is a handsome perennial growing to about 4ft (1.2m) tall with a spread of 2ft (60cm). The flowers, similar to those of the lupine (*Lupinus*) but more sparsely carried on the gray-green stems, are borne in summer and are a rich, deep blue, sometimes flecked with white or cream. Dark gray seedpods follow the flowers in the fall. The leaves are mid- to deep green and are made up of lance-shaped leaflets. White false indigo (*B. alba*) is similar but has pure white flowers.

False indigo (*B. lactea*, syn. *B. leucantha*) grows to 5ft (1.5m) or more in height and its white flowers are held on branching stems in late spring to summer. It is found in moist ground in the wild from Virginia to Florida.

WHERE TO PLANT

Blue false indigo and white false indigo prefer a position in full sun and sandy, open soil that is free from lime. False indigo prefers deeper, richer, moister soil in sun.

PLANT CARE

Sow ripe seed in autumn. Divide established plants in early spring once they are three to four years old; otherwise, do not disturb the roots. All species are trouble-free.

PLANTING SUGGESTIONS

Because false indigo tends to flower fairly early in the year, plant it where the foliage will be obscured by late-flowering plants, or with a plant whose foliage will outgrow it.

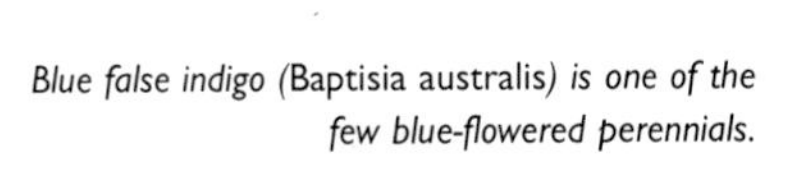

*Blue false indigo (*Baptisia australis*) is one of the few blue-flowered perennials.*

Boltonia asteroides

ASTERACEAE/COMPOSITAE

False chamomile

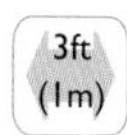

This herbaceous perennial belongs to a genus containing about 10 species that originate in North America, where they are found in moist soil in full sun.

This species closely resembles the New York Aster (*Aster novi-belgii*), with its small flowerheads of many daisylike, white, mauve or pinkish-purple flowers with golden-yellow eyes; flowers appear from late summer to mid-autumn. The leaves are bluish green, long and lance-shaped, and they are positioned alternately up the tall, branching stems, which can reach 7ft (2.2m). The cultivar 'Snowbank' has pure white flowers and grows to the same height and spread as the species.

Boltonia asteroides var. *latisquama* (syn. *B. latisquama*), a somewhat smaller variety, grows to about 5ft (1.5m) high but has larger flowers in deep lilac or white. It is native to the eastern and central U.S.

WHERE TO PLANT

Grow false chamomile in fertile, moist, well-drained soil. They do best in full sun but will cope with partial shade.

PLANT CARE

Divide plants every two or three years in spring to maintain vigor. Stake tall plants. To propagate, sow seed in autumn or divide established clumps in early spring. Like many members of the aster genus, false chamomile is susceptible to mildew but is otherwise trouble-free.

PLANTING SUGGESTIONS

False chamomiles are most effective when they are grown in natural-looking drifts within a mixed border. Plant them with New York asters to provide flowers over a long period from spring to mid-autumn.

If you want a profusion of daisylike flowers, Boltonia asteroides *is the plant for you. It will produce an eye-catching tall display of pinkish white flowers with noticeable golden eyes from late summer to mid autumn.*

Campanula

CAMPANULACEAE

Bellflower

This genus is huge, with 300 species of annuals, biennials, and perennials making up its numbers. They range from mat-forming alpine species to large herbaceous perennials, but only a couple can be called "giant." These are milky bellflower (*Campanula lactiflora*), which grows to 5ft (1.5m) with a spread of 2ft (60cm), and the appropriately named chimney bellflower (*C. pyramidalis*), which towers over *C. lactiflora* at 10ft (3m).

The hardy *C. lactiflora* (zones 4–8) has cone-shaped panicles of bell-shaped flowers in white or shades of blue or violet. They are ½in–1in (1–2.5cm) across and are borne on branching stems over a long season from early summer to early fall. The leaves are mid-green, long and oval, with toothed edges.

C. latifolia, which is often (but misleadingly, in this context) called the giant bellflower, is large and vigorous, and it usually gets to heights of about 4ft (1.2m).

WHERE TO PLANT

C. lactiflora and *C. pyramidalis* and their cultivars like fairly similar conditions, doing best in fertile, moist, slightly alkaline soil. While they will cope with full sun, their preference is for partial shade.

PLANT CARE

You will need to stake the plants to prevent stems from leaning or toppling over. Deadheading bellflowers after the first flush of flowers will encourage a second flush of smaller ones to form. Bellflowers may be attacked by slugs and snails and also by aphids. Mildew and rust can also be a problem, especially when the soil dries out.

PLANTING SUGGESTIONS

Grow these bellflowers at the back of a border or in drifts of similar large perennials such as foxgloves (*Digitalis*) in a natural planting scheme. They are lovely additions to a wildflower garden.

Campanulas are eye-catching plants with a long flowering season.

Cardiocrinum

LILIACEAE

Giant lily

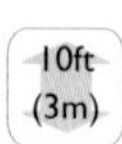

This genus contains just three species of giant lily, which are native to the forests of Japan, China, and the Himalayas. Everything about the best-known species, *Cardiocrinum giganteum* (formerly *Lilium giganteum*), is large. It is a bulbous perennial that has as many as 20 huge, trumpet-shaped, strongly-scented flowers, each up to 9in (23cm) long. The flowers are a creamy white with maroon stripes on the inside of the trumpet and are borne on erect stems. The leaves are about 18in (45cm) long and form basal rosettes; they are dark green, glossy, and oval in shape. The stems, leaves and young shoots of *C. giganteum* var. *yunnanense* are tinged bronze-purple, and the flowers have a greenish tinge.

The smaller *C. cordatum* (syn. *Lilium cordatum*) grows to 6ft (1.8m) tall. Its dark green leaves are about 12in (30cm) long and the cream-colored, fragrant flowers are up to 6in (15cm) long.

WHERE TO PLANT

Giant lilies grow best in damp, partially shaded woodland. They will do best if the soil is not allowed to get too wet, but it must never be allowed to dry out altogether.

PLANT CARE

Plant the bulbs in groups, just below the soil's surface in deep, fertile (but not waterlogged) soil. Keep feeding throughout the growing season to encourage the formation of bulblets, from which they can most successfully be propagated; however, you can also sow ripe seeds in autumn. Stake the shoots and feed with a seaweed-based fertilizer a couple of times during the growing season. Mulch in winter. Slugs may damage young shoots. Bulbs may take several years before they start to flower.

PLANTING SUGGESTIONS

Plant bulbs in small groups with space around them so that the leaves are not crowded out.

Exquisite, lily-like flowers distinguish the mammoth giant lily (Cardiocrinum giganteum).

Cephalaria

DIPSACACEAE

Cephalaria

There are some 65 species of annuals and perennials in this genus, which occur naturally in Asia, Africa and Europe. Two of the biggest species are yellow cephalaria (*Cephalaria alpina*, formerly *Scabiosa alpina*), which grows up to 6ft (1.8m) tall, and giant cephalaria (*C. gigantea*, formerly *Scabiosa gigantea*), which is even bigger, growing up to 8ft (2.5m). They both have the typical scabious leaves, pinnate and toothed, and the equally typical flowers, usually described as pincushion-like, but with sulfur-yellow or white petals surrounding a central boss of stamens. There is not a great deal of difference between the two, but giant cephalaria has larger leaves, up to 16in (40cm) long, and larger flowers, up to 2in (6cm) across.

WHERE TO PLANT

Both species do best in moist, fertile soil and they will cope with sun or partial shade.

PLANT CARE

In exposed gardens, the tall stems will need staking, but these plants are otherwise trouble-free. To propagate, divide established clumps in early spring or sow seed in spring.

PLANTING SUGGESTIONS

Grow these large, rather imposing plants at the back of a large border or in natural drifts with other tall perennials such as tickseed (*Coreopsis*) and goat's rue (*Galega*). They will look best if they have room to spread, so do not overcrowd them with other plants of equal height.

*This exceptionally large giant cephalaria (*Cephalaria gigantea*) enjoys moist, fertile soil.*

Clematis

RANUNCULACEAE

Clematis

There is a great variety of clematis to choose from, but only a few of the species and cultivars that cover the greatest area and are the most vigorous are included here.

Clematis are divided into three groups, based on growth type and blossoming time. Evergreen clematis (*Clematis armandii*, Group 1) has the bonus of scented flowers. Growing to about 15ft (5m), it flowers in early spring in a profusion of saucer-shaped, scented, white flowers, each about 2in (5cm) across. Its leaves are slender, dark green and slightly waxy. *C. armandii* 'Apple Blossom' has pale pink flowers.

Anemone clematis (*C. montana*, Group 1) is an especially vigorous species. It flowers from late spring to early summer, producing white, single flowers about 2in (5cm) in diameter. *C. montana* var. *rubens* 'Elizabeth' is a popular cultivar with pale pink flowers. *C. montana* f. *grandiflora* is even more vigorous than the species, and has large, white flowers with cream anthers; the flowers grow up to 4in (10cm) across and the plant will reach a height of 30ft (10m) or so. *C. montana* var. *rubens* is also vigorous, reaching similar heights. It has pale to deep pink flowers with prominent yellow anthers. Golden clematis (*C. tangutica*, Group 3) flowers in autumn. The unusual pale yellow, bell-shaped flowers are followed by striking fluffy seedheads. It is also vigorous and will reach heights of 20ft (6m).

WHERE TO PLANT

Although hybrid clematis tend to prefer a warm, sunny spot, anemone clematis will cope well with a north-facing wall. Plant all clematis with their roots in fertile, reliably moist, well-drained soil in shade, with the top of the rootball well below the surface of the soil—about 3in (8cm) is ideal; this will encourage shoots to form below soil level, which provides some protection against clematis wilt, the scourge of all clematis.

Opposite: Clematis *'Crimson King' is seen here mingling with escallonia.*

PLANT CARE

Cut back newly planted clematis to a couple of buds 12in (30cm) or so above ground level, and as new shoots develop, tie them gently to a system of horizontal wires. Pruning will vary according to the type of clematis. Group 1 clematis (early-flowering species and cultivars) are pruned immediately after flowering, when shoots can be shortened by about one-third of their length. Group 2 clematis (early-flowering, large-flowered cultivars) and Group 3 clematis (late-flowering, large-flowered cultivars, late-flowering species, and small-flowered cultivars) are pruned in early spring, when the previous year's growth should be cut back to a pair of strong buds about 12in (30cm) above ground level.

The major problem is clematis wilt, but planting new plants well below the surface of the soil often enables them to stage a comeback, even though the plant appears to have died.

PLANTING SUGGESTIONS

Anemone clematis will scramble happily over old tree stumps, but all clematis described here are vigorous and need sturdy supports.

Above: Clematis montana *var.* rubens *is, deservedly, one of the most popular clematis.*

Coreopsis

ASTERACEAE/COMPOSITAE

Tickseed

There is a wide range of annuals and perennials in the genus *Coreopsis*, but only one—tall tickseed (*Coreopsis tripteris*), which grows to 6ft (1.8m)—qualifies for inclusion in this book. These plants originate in the prairies and woodlands of North and Central America. They have large heads of lemon-yellow daisylike flowers that are borne on long stems from mid- to late summer. The leaves are mid-green, either lance-shaped or pinnate, and about 4in (10cm) long.

WHERE TO PLANT

Grow tall tickseed in fertile, well-drained soil. Plants will do well in sun or partial shade.

PLANT CARE

The delicate, slightly brittle stems require support, particularly in windy situations. If you deadhead the flowers, you will prolong the blooming season. To propagate, sow seeds in mid-autumn for plants that flower the following year. You can also propagate tall tickseed from basal root cuttings in spring or by dividing established plants in spring. Plants are susceptible to damage by slugs and snails but are otherwise trouble-free.

PLANTING SUGGESTIONS

Tall tickseed looks lovely in an herbaceous border with late-flowering dahlias and chrysanthemums to extend the flowering season. They are also suitable for individual containers in a tiered display with other members of the genus.

The slightly smaller annual coreopsis (*C. tinctoria*, syn. *Calliopsis tinctoria*), for example, is similar but has bright yellow flowers, and there are cultivars to be found with flowers in shades of dark reds and purple, some of them dwarf. Coreopsis flowers are attractive to bees.

*The bright yellow flowers of tickseed (*Coreopsis*) make a welcome splash of color in the summer border.*

Cortaderia selloana

POACEAE/GRAMINEAE

Pampas grass

An evergreen perennial, pampas grass (*Cortaderia selloana*) originates, as you might expect from the name, in South America's plains. One of the giant grasses, in late summer its striking silvery plumes tower above the arching, waxy green leaves. Each plume can grow up to 8ft (2.5m) long and are borne together in large, dense tufts.

There are a number of cultivars. *C. selloana* 'Albolineata' (also known as 'Silver Stripe') (zones 8–9) has white-edged leaves and white plumes; it is altogether a more compact plant, better suited to smaller gardens, as it grows to 6ft (1.8m). 'Aureolineata' (syn. 'Gold Band') (zones 7–9) is slightly taller, at 7ft (2.2m), and has gold-edged leaves. 'Sunningdale Silver' (zones 8–9) is a true giant, growing to 10ft (3m) with silvery plumes. It is also tough, but much less hardy than other green-leafed cultivars.

WHERE TO PLANT

Pampas grass needs fertile, well-drained soil and full sun.

PLANT CARE

You will need to protect young plants in their first winter by covering the crowns with straw unless you are in Zone 9 or warmer regions, or are planting a hardier clone. In late winter, remove the old foliage and the previous year's stems. Divide clumps in spring to propagate new plants, or sow seeds in warmth in spring. Pampas grass is generally known to be pest- and disease-free.

PLANTING SUGGESTIONS

Pampas grass is a focal point in its own right. Grow the large forms as free-standing specimens with plenty of room. Smaller forms with other tall grasses can be planted at the back of a border.

*Pampas grass (*Cortaderia selloana*), with its eye-catching silvery plumes, makes a giant architectural feature.*

Crambe cordifolia

BRASSICACEAE/CRUCIFERAE

Colewort

 Z 6–9
 8ft (2.5m)
 5ft (1.5m)

One of the largest perennials, colewort (*Crambe cordifolia*) is one of some 20 species of annuals and perennials from seaside areas and open grassland in Central Asia. It has large, soft green leaves, surmounted by thick stems which either have small leaves or are leafless. Tiny, scented, starry, white flowers are borne in large panicles that float above the plant. The flowers last from late spring to midsummer and can form clumps up to 5ft (1.5m) across.

WHERE TO PLANT

Colewort does best in fertile, alkaline soil in full sun. It will cope with poorer soil and shadier conditions, but will not grow as tall.

PLANT CARE

Protect plants from strong winds. Propagate from root cuttings taken in winter or from seed sown in autumn or spring. Established colewort is subject to the usual diseases of the cabbage family, including clubroot.

PLANTING SUGGESTIONS

Plant as a stunning backdrop to a summer border, particularly an all-white one.

*Colewort (*Crambe cordifolia*) is a great back-of-the-border plant, with its clouds of starry, white flowers.*

Cynara

ASTERACEAE/COMPOSITAE

Cardoon, Globe artichoke

 Z 7–9
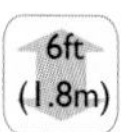 6ft (1.8m)
 4ft (1.2m)

There are about 11 species of these large, thistlelike perennials in the genus. Many of them make handsome architectural plants, but the most commonly grown in gardens is cardoon (*Cynara cardunculus*), and its variant, globe artichoke (*Cardunculus* Scolymus Group). Both grow to 3–6ft (1–1.8m). They bear silvery gray, armadillo-like flower buds, and in summer to early autumn these explode into purple, thistlelike flowerheads. The deeply lobed, silver-gray leaves of both species are between 18in and 3ft (45cm–1m) long.

WHERE TO PLANT

Grow both species in moist, well-drained soil in full sun, ideally sheltered from strong winds.

PLANT CARE

The flower buds of globe artichokes and cardoons can be eaten as vegetables, but if you are growing these plants for their handsome foliage, it pays to remove the flowerheads as they form. In cold areas, mulch the base of the plants in winter with straw. It is easiest to propagate these perennials by dividing established clumps. Alternatively, take root cuttings in winter or sow seed in spring. Both species are generally trouble-free, but they can be damaged by slugs and aphids, and they are sometimes affected by gray mold (botrytis). They are also damaged by mirid (capsid) bugs which mar the upper leaves and flowers.

PLANTING SUGGESTIONS

Grow cardoons and globe artichokes at the back of an herbaceous border, as the central feature plant in an island bed, or as an architectural plant in a large pot—choose a container at least 18in (45cm) in diameter.

Globe artichokes and cardoons can be planted with other silver leafed foliage plants for a silver border, or accented with blues.

Delphinium

RANUNCULACEAE

Delphinium

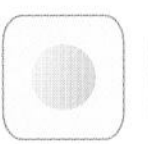

With their glorious range of rich colors and striking spires of flowers, delphiniums are among the most eye-catching of giant perennials and among the most popular. They need little introduction to most gardeners, but it may come as a surprise to learn that this genus of more than 300 species includes annuals and biennials, as well as perennials.

Perennial delphinium cultivars are divided into three principal groups. The tallest are those belonging to the Elatum Group, and some of these reach well over 6ft (1.8m). The other two groups are Belladonna, which are smaller with a more branching shape and single flowers, and Pacific hybrids, which are grown as annuals or biennials and reach a height of about 5ft (1.5m). There are also large-flowered hybrids, usually with delphiniums from the Elatum Group as one of the parents that range in height from 4–8ft (1.2–2.5m).

The color range of delphiniums runs from creamy white to pink and violet to the more traditional blues—pale blue, mid-blue and royal blue. The flowers grow in spires with a cup-shaped, sometimes hooded, spurred form, and they can be single or double. In his classic book, *Perennial Garden Plants* (1976), Graham Stuart Thomas describes the flowers as "elfin bonnets." If deadheaded regularly, delphiniums can bloom from early to late summer. The leaves are large, toothed and have three, five or seven lobes.

There are many excellent cultivars; the following are all in the Elatum Group: *D.* 'Bruce' has semi-double, violet-blue flowers and grows to 6ft (1.8m); *D.* 'Fanfare', a gigantic plant at 7ft (2.2m) tall, has light mauve flowers with white eyes.

WHERE TO PLANT

Delphiniums need a sunny site and rich, fertile soil, but, most importantly, they need shelter from strong winds.

There are many hybrid delphiniums to choose from. Those from the Elatum Group are among the largest.

PLANT CARE

The delicate stems of tall delphiniums must be staked. Start doing so when the plants reach about 12in (30cm) in height, using stout stakes and garden string. If you thin out the shoots to a maximum of five on each plant, you will ensure good, strong flowerheads. Deadhead the flower spires as they fade to allow younger shoots to replace them. Cut back to ground level in autumn.

You can propagate delphiniums by taking basal cuttings of perennial groups in early spring. Annuals can be sown from seed in warmth in early spring. Unfortunately, delphiniums are particularly attractive to slugs and snails and they are also prone to mildews and leaf miners.

PLANTING SUGGESTIONS

Put the tallest delphiniums at the back of a border, or in the center of an island bed. Plant in groups of at least three or more, and opt for odd-numbered groups—three, five or seven, etc.—to create a natural-looking effect. Try planting bright blue delphiniums with yellow meadow rue (*Thalictrum flavum* ssp. *glaucum*, syn. *T. speciosissimum*), which has blue-green glaucous leaves.

Delphinium *'Blue Jade' has tall spires of large blue flowers from early summer onwards.*

Dierama pulcherrimum

IRIDACEAE

Angels'-fishing-rods, wandflower

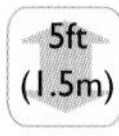

Dierama pulcherrimum, which grows from a corm, scrapes in at the lower end of the "giant" spectrum, but its slender growth habit gives it the appearance of being taller than it is. It is one of about 40 species of evergreen cormous perennials that hail from moist mountainous areas of Africa, and it produces tufts of long, slender, grassy, gray-green leaves. The slightly drooping, tubular bell-shaped, purplish pink flowers are borne on long, arching stems that rise above the leaves (hence the angels'-fishing-rod sobriquet). The cultivar 'Blackbird' has deep purple flowers.

Another species, grassybells (*Dierama pendulum*), could more truly be called "giant" but is less commonly grown. It is similar to angels'-fishing-rods, but the flowers are more open, although still bell-shaped.

WHERE TO PLANT

In spring, plant the corms about 3in (8cm) deep in well-drained soil to which plenty of humus has been added. Alternatively, where colder, start them in containers in warmth. Give the plants shelter from cold winds, and site them in full sun.

PLANT CARE

Each year the plant will form new corms on top of the old ones, but angels'-fishing-rods are slow to establish and dislike being disturbed, so only dig up and divide clumps when they are obviously overcrowded. Plants can be divided in spring, or ripe seeds can be sown in autumn. Make sure you water the plants well during the growing season. Once established, they are usually trouble-free.

PLANTING SUGGESTIONS

Grow angels'-fishing-rods toward the back of the border in a purple-, pink- and blue-themed planting scheme or around the perimeter of a pond. A shorter species, *D. luteoalbidum*, which grows to about 3ft (1m) tall, has cream or white flowers and can be used closer to the front of the border.

*Undeniably elegant, the wandflower (*Dierama pulcherrimum*) has delicate, purplish-pink flowers on long, arching stems.*

Digitalis

SCROPHULARIACEAE

Foxglove

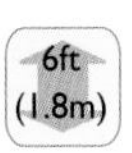

Foxgloves are short-lived perennials and biennials that originate in temperate regions in Europe, north Africa, and central Asia. They are generally found in open woodlands and are notable for their tall spires, which are packed with distinctive tubular, bell-shaped flowers with freckled markings on the inside. They have medicinal properties (used for heart conditions) and can cause acute discomfort if eaten. The foliage can be a skin irritant.

Although there are several other species in the genus, the well-known common foxglove (*Digitalis purpurea*), with its spires of pink, purple or white flowers, is the tallest at 6ft (1.8m). *D. purpurea* f. *albiflora* has lovely pure white flowers (or white with colored spotting in the throat) in early summer and the typical large, soft, slightly toothed, dark green leaves. *D. purpurea* Excelsior Group are an imposing group, with variously colored flowers. *D. purpurea* Gloxinioides Group has frilly-edged flowers in a range of colors, from salmon pink to soft yellow, purple and pink, all of which are heavily spotted on the insides. *D. purpurea* 'Sutton's Apricot', which is among the tallest, has soft orange-colored flowers.

WHERE TO PLANT

Foxgloves do best in partial shade in humus-rich soil.

PLANT CARE

Robust, upright plants, foxgloves do not require staking. In the right conditions, they will self-seed to form extensive colonies, so deadhead after flowering if you want to prevent this. Sow fresh seed in late spring *in situ*. Foxgloves are generally trouble-free, although powdery mildew and leaf spot can occur.

PLANTING SUGGESTIONS

Grow in a slightly shaded border or under a light tree canopy.

Excelsior Group foxgloves (Digitalis purpurea *Excelsior Group) come in a range of exquisite colors.*

Dryopteris

ASPIDIACEAE/DRYOPTERIDACEAE

Wood fern, Shield fern

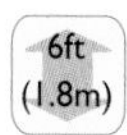

There are some 225 species of woodfern, but only a few are really large and the only giant is the herbaceous alpine Wallich's wood fern (*Dryopteris wallichiana*) (zones 6–8), which comes from the Himalayas and grows to 6ft (1.8m) in the right conditions. It produces a long, erect shuttlecock of dark green fronds that are yellowish-green when young.

WHERE TO PLANT

Wood fern prefers reliably moist, humus-rich soil and a shady, sheltered position. Dig in plenty of humus before you plant.

PLANT CARE

To propagate, sow the spores in warmth when ripe, or divide mature clumps of plants in spring. Ferns are generally easy-going plants that are more or less trouble-free.

PLANTING SUGGESTIONS

Grow several ferns together in a shaded location to make a small "fernery."

Dryopteris *spp. are well-suited to a shady and sheltered location.*

Echinops

ASTERACEAE/COMPOSITAE

Globe thistle

The globe thistle originates in mountainous regions in hot parts of the world, notably India and Africa. There are some seriously big contenders in this genus, the biggest being the appropriately named *Echinops giganteus* (zones 7–9/half-hardy), which grows to a massive 15ft (5m). The long, bristly, deeply-lobed leaves have thick white hairs on their undersides and are silvery gray-green on their upper sides. Large, spherical, gray-blue flowerheads, up to 9in (23cm) in diameter, are produced in summer.

Smaller but still imposing at 6ft (1.8m) is the great globe thistle (*E. sphaerocephalus*) (zones 3–8), which has similarly spiny, gray-green leaves and smaller, silver-gray flowerheads slightly later in the summer. They are borne on thick silvery stems.

WHERE TO PLANT

These big thistles prefer a dry, sunny spot in poor soil, as befits their mountainous origins, but they are not fussy and will cope well in most conditions, including partial shade.

PLANT CARE

Globe thistles can be invasive if left to self-seed, so remove the flowerheads before the seeds form. Sow fresh seeds in spring or divide established clumps in autumn or early spring. They are generally trouble-free plants but can be susceptible to attacks by aphids (capsids), and leaf miners.

PLANTING SUGGESTIONS

These are ideal plants for the back of a sunny border, but they can also be used as the central feature in an island bed or as an architectural feature, providing a good focal point in a gravel garden, for example.

*The globe thistle (*Echinops*) is a remarkable plant.* E. bannaticus *'Taplow Blue' has striking blue flowers.*

Epilobium angustifolium

ONAGRACEAE

Fireweed, Rosebay willow herb

This genus contains a large variety of annuals, biennials, herbaceous and semi-evergreen perennials, and some subshrubs. They are good survivors, being widely distributed over the temperate regions of the world, where they are often found on waste ground, along roadsides and on gravelly slopes. Some spread rapidly by means of stolons to form groundcover, but there are selections to be found which are non-invasive. The species is usually represented in gardens by the variety *Epilobium angustifolium* var. *album* (syn. *Chamerion angustifolium* var. *album*), which is a vigorously spreading, rhizomatous perennial distinguished by its erect plumes of saucer-shaped, white flowers with green sepals. The leaves are pale to mid-green and willow-like.

WHERE TO PLANT

Grow fireweed in moist, well-drained soil, in full sun or partial shade.

PLANT CARE

If you do not want the plants to self-seed, dead-head them regularly, which will also encourage a longer flowering season. As they self-seed, they will propagate themselves. Move the young seedlings to where you want them to grow. Fireweed is susceptible to rusts and mildews and is vulnerable to attacks by slugs and snails.

PLANTING SUGGESTIONS

The stately plumes look best with other perennials in natural drifts in semi-wild areas of the garden.

*Of the fireweeds (*Epilobium angustifolium*), the white variety album is the most distinguished looking.*

Eremurus

ASPHODELACEAE/LILIACEAE

Eremurus

In this genus of some 45 or so species of perennials originating in dry regions of Asia, the foxtail lily is recognizable by its tall spires of small, star-shaped flowers with conspicuous stamens, which appear from late spring to midsummer. The spires of white, pink or yellow flowers rise from a basal rosette of leaves.

Eremurus himalaicus (zones 5–8) grows up to 6ft (1.8m) tall and has long "tails" of starry white flowers and a clump of strap-shaped, bright green leaves that can be more than 2ft (60cm) long. *E. robustus* (zones 5–8) has longer, bluish-green leaves up to 3ft (1m), and a spire of pale pink flowers with yellow stamens. The cultivars of *E.* x *isabellinus* (zones 6–9) are similarly tall, with flowers in a range of colors; 'Firecracker', for example, has bright orange flowers.

WHERE TO PLANT

Foxtail lilies do well in sandy soil that has been enriched with humus. They prefer to be sheltered in a sunny spot.

PLANT CARE

When they are grown on exposed sites, foxtail lilies will need to be supported. It is a good idea to mulch the crowns in autumn and winter with straw, because the young growth can be damaged by frosts. Propagate from seed sown in warmth in autumn, or divide established clumps after flowering. Young plants are susceptible to slugs, but these plants are otherwise trouble-free.

PLANTING SUGGESTIONS

Foxtail lilies combine well with other dry-loving perennials, such as thistles (*Onopordum*), mulleins (*Verbascum*) and poppies (*Meconopsis*).

E. stenophyllus (zones 6–9) has rich golden-yellow flowers above gray-green leaves. Plant with its taller cousins to provide variation in height in a mixed border.

The spires of foxtail lily (*Eremurus himalaicus*) are definitely larger than life!

Eryngium

APIACEAE/UMBELLIFERAE

Eryngo

The large number of annuals, biennials and perennials in this genus fall into two distinct groups—those that originate from the dry, rocky areas of Europe, North Africa and Asia, and those that originate from Central and South America. The former group are tap-rooted, dry-loving plants with conspicuous flowers. The latter are fibrous-rooted plants with smaller, greenish-white or purplish-brown flowers.

Eryngium agavifolium (zones 6–10) belongs to the second group. It has evergreen, sword-shaped, sharply-toothed, glossy foliage and branching heads of small, thistlelike, greenish-white flowers in late summer. It grows up to 5ft (1.5m) tall.

E. eburneum (zones 8–10), also from the second group, prefers moist soil. It has large evergreen leaves, up to 3ft (lm) long, and branching heads of greenish-white flowers with spiny bracts in late summer. It also grows to about 5ft (1.5m) tall with a spread of about 2ft (60cm).

The bruiser in the group is *E. pandanifolium* (zones 8–10), which can get to 13ft (4m) tall and 6ft (1.8m) across. An evergreen perennial, it comes from South America and belongs to the group preferring moist soil. The large, silvery, sword-shaped leaves can be up to 6ft (1.8m) long, and the purplish-brown flowers are borne in clusters late in the year.

WHERE TO PLANT

Grow *E. agavifolium* in dry soil in a sunny spot, and make sure that the plants do not get waterlogged in winter. *E. eburneum* and *E. pandanifolium* need moisture-retentive, well-drained soil and full sun.

PLANT CARE

Both types of eryngo can be propagated from root cuttings in late winter. Alternatively, divide clumps of established plants in spring. They are susceptible to powdery mildew and to slug and snail predation.

PLANTING SUGGESTIONS

Grow these large plants at the back of a border according to soil preference. They look particularly good with other tall plants, such as colewort (*Crambe cordifolia*) and plume poppy (*Macleaya cordata*). They also combine well with some of the smaller eryngos, especially the popular and reliably hardy *E. giganteum*, which is commonly known as Miss Willmott's ghost, after an Edwardian gardener who used to scatter the seeds surreptitiously in gardens she visited. It will grow up to 4ft (l.2m) tall and to about 12in (30cm) across, and it produces handsome, large, steel blue flowers surrounded by prominent prickly bracts.

Although not the tallest Eryngium, *the sputnik-like flower spikes of* Eryngium giganteum *make a striking addition to a dry garden.*

Eupatorium

ASTERACEAE/COMPOSITAE

Joe Pye weed, Hemp agrimony, Dog fennel

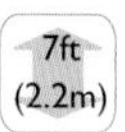

This genus includes about 40 annuals, perennials, shrubs, and subshrubs. They are mostly vigorous plants from a diverse range of habitats, ranging from swamps to dry sandy areas. The flowers produce plenty of nectar and are attractive to both bees and butterflies. Among the larger perennials in the group is Joe Pye weed (*Eupatorium purpureum*) (zones 3–9). The tall stems are surrounded by long, pointed, mid-green, purple-tinged leaves and are surmounted by dense clusters of pinkish purple or creamy white flowers; the flowers are borne over a long period from summer to early fall. Plants grow up to 7ft (2.2m) tall and form good clumps.

There are two other large perennials in the group. Hemp agrimony (*E. cannabinum*) (zones 3–9) grows to about 5ft (1.5m) and has toothed, lance-shaped leaves and large clusters of purple, pink or white flowers from summer to autumn. The dog fennel (*E. capillifolium* 'Elegant Feather') (zones 6–10) has delicate stems that are covered in bright green filigree-like foliage, making it quite unlike other species in the genus. The flowers, which are insignificant, appear in late autumn.

WHERE TO PLANT

Grow these plants in good soil in sun or in partial shade.

PLANT CARE

The stems of these plants are strong and do not normally require staking. Sow seed in autumn or divide clumps in spring. They are generally free of pests and diseases.

PLANTING SUGGESTIONS

Include eupatoriums in a bee and butterfly border along with lavender (*Lavandula*), rosemary (*Rosmarinus*), butterfly bush (*Buddleja*), lavender cotton (*Santolina*) and heliotrope (*Heliotropium*), or plant it in drifts with large asters and other plants with daisylike flowers.

*Above: A great plant for large drifts, Joe Pye weed (*Eupatorium purpureum*) is an excellent candidate for the wild garden.*

Right: In closeup, E. p. subsp. maculatum *'Atropurpureum' with its dark-colored stems.*

Euphorbia

EUPHORBIACEAE

Spurge

This large and diverse genus encompasses many hundreds of annuals, biennials, evergreen and semi-evergreen perennials, shrubs, trees and succulents. Many have unusual flowers in which the bracts (modified leaves) form the most eye-catching element. They are notorious for their milky sap, which can be a skin irritant.

Euphorbia characias subsp. *wulfenii*, sometimes classified as a shrub, originates in the Mediterranean region. It will make an imposing, spreading clump, with the stems covered in narrow, bluish-gray leaves and bearing flower spikes composed largely of yellowish green bracts.

WHERE TO PLANT

Spurge does best in light, sandy soil in full sun.

PLANT CARE

Sow seeds either when ripe in autumn or in spring. Basal cuttings can be taken in spring or early summer. Spurge can suffer from gray mold (botrytis), and they are sometimes infested with aphids. The main cause of plant failure is root rock. To avoid this, usually from planting pot-bound plants, be sure to spread out a plant's roots to enable it to take hold in the ground.

PLANTING SUGGESTIONS

E. characias is a good choice for a large pot, and a matching pair on each side of a gateway or path makes a bold statement.

Another large spurge, *E. sikkimensis* (zones 6–9) is a hardy herbaceous perennial and grows to 4ft (1.2m). It has bright green leaves, pinkish young shoots, and chrome yellow flower bracts. It prefers moist soil in light shade, and is useful for providing structure in a mixed border.

The ever-popular Euphorbia characias *subsp.* wulfenii *is a striking addition to a dry garden.*

Ferula communis

APIACEAE/UMBELLIFERAE

Giant fennel

The genus *Ferula* contains more than 170 species, of which the most commonly grown is the herbaceous perennial giant fennel (*Ferula communis*). Although it is called giant "fennel," it is quite different from the culinary sweet fennel (*Foeniculum vulgare*). Giant fennel was discovered in North Africa in the 17th century and is also native to rough, rocky ground in other Mediterranean countries. It makes a truly striking impression with its lacelike, finely dissected, greenish yellow foliage. Throughout summer, an immensely tall, stout, erect stem bears aloft branching, cow-parsley-like flowers that are buttery yellow.

F. tingitana is similar but taller, sometimes growing to 10ft (3m) or more.

WHERE TO PLANT

Grow in fairly rich, well-drained soil in full sun.

PLANT CARE

In very cold climates, protect the crowns with a mulch of straw or twigs in winter. To propagate, sow seeds when ripe, pricking out seedlings into deeper containers to allow the long tap-roots to develop. Giant fennel will self-seed quite freely, but it does not recover well from transplanting. Giant fennel can take several years to flower and may die after seeding. Plants are susceptible to aphids and to slug and snail damage, and mildew can also be a problem.

PLANTING SUGGESTIONS

Grow giant fennel as a feature plant or with other really large perennials, such as tall thistles (*Echinops*) and colewort (*Crambe cordifolia*).

*The giant fennel (*Ferula communis*) produces ethereal heads of yellowish-green flowers.*

Filipendula rubra

ROSACEAE

Queen of the prairie

Most of the species in the genus *Filipendula* originate in damp, boggy areas in northern temperate regions, and queen of the prairie (*Filipendula rubra*), native to the eastern states of the U.S. is no exception. It is a tough, vigorous perennial with handsome foliage of deeply lobed, mid-green leaves up to 8in (20cm) across. The dark red flower stalks bear branching heads topped with clusters of pink, scented flowers from early summer onward. Martha Washington's plume (*F. r.* 'Venusta') has dark pink flowers.

WHERE TO PLANT

Plant in late fall or early spring in moist, well-drained, fairly rich soil in sun or semi-shade.

PLANT CARE

Cut back the top growth as it dies back in autumn. Propagate from root cuttings in early spring or divide established clumps in spring or autumn. Plants will be more susceptible to problems if the soil is too dry, when fungal leaf spot and mildew can be a problem. In reliably moist soil, however, it will make a resilient, large, spreading clump.

PLANTING SUGGESTIONS

Queen of the prairie is a good subject for a bog garden or for the damp soil near the edge of a natural pool. It is also an attractive addition to a wild garden. *F. purpurea* f. *albiflora* (zones 4–9) is smaller, at 4ft (1.2m), but its frothy heads of white flowers combine well with *F. rubra.*

*Queen of the prairie (*Filipendula rubra*) is a vigorous perennial; it is ideally suited for wild gardens, where it will form large drifts.*

Foeniculum vulgare

APIACEAE/UMBELLIFERAE

Sweet fennel

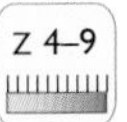

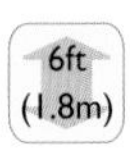

There is only one species in this genus. Fennel has finely dissected, almost feathery, mid-green foliage with an aniseed-like scent and large, rather flat heads of yellow flowers borne on widely branching stems in mid- to late summer. The flowers are followed by the highly aromatic seeds. There are a couple of good cultivars: *F. vulgare* 'Giant Bronze', and *F. vulgare* 'Purpureum' (syn. 'Bronze').

WHERE TO PLANT

Fennel is a deep-rooted plant and does best in fertile, moist, well-drained soil in full sun.

PLANT CARE

The stems are tough and sturdy enough not to require staking. You can sow the seeds indoors in warmth in early spring or *in situ* in late spring. Thin seedlings out to a distance of 2ft (60cm) or so, or transplant self-sown seedlings when they are about 4in (10cm) high. Plants can be susceptible to aphid and slug attacks and to mildew.

PLANTING SUGGESTIONS

Plant as the centerpiece in an ornamental potager or at the back of a border.

*Sweet fennel (*Foeniculum vulgare*) is an herb with delicate foliage and beautiful yellowish-green umbels of flowers.*

Fritillaria imperialis

LILIACEAE

Crown imperial, Fritillary

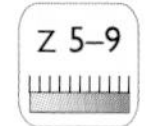

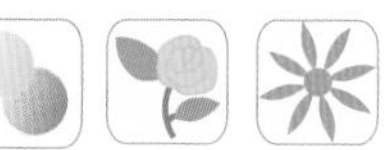

There are about 100 species of bulbous perennials in the genus *Fritillaria*, some from around the Mediterranean and others from Asia and North America, but only one of them can be described as giant: the aptly named crown imperial fritillary (*Fritillaria imperialis*). It is an unusual and striking-looking plant, and it can be found in the wild from Turkey to Kashmir.

In early summer, the tall, dark stems arise from whorls of bright green, glossy, strappy leaves and bear aloft clusters of bright orange, yellow, or red, bell-shaped, drooping flowers that are surmounted by a tuft of leaf-like green bracts (the crown). A foxy odor emanates from the plant, which some people find unpleasant. There are a number of cultivars: 'Lutea' has bright yellow flowers; 'The Premier' has orange-yellow flowers with purple markings.

WHERE TO GROW

Crown imperials do best in full sun or partial shade, in fertile, well-drained soils. The bulbs should be planted deep (about four times their own depth), with extra grit in the planting hole to improve drainage.

PLANT CARE

These fritillaries do best when they are well watered in spring but left fairly dry in the summer months. Divide offsets and plant them in late summer. Fritillaries are susceptible to lily beetle and can be damaged by slugs.

PLANTING SUGGESTIONS

Use these imposing bulbs as a container plant or in a border with torch lilies (*Kniphofia*) and alliums (*Allium*).

*With its "crowns" of bracts, crown imperial fritillary (*Fritillaria imperialis*) makes a striking feature in early summer.*

Galega

LEGUMINOSAE/PAPILIONACEAE

Goat's rue, French lilac

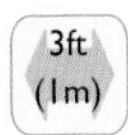

There are only six species in this genus of easy-going, vigorous perennials, which are found in the meadows of central Europe and the mountains of Africa. They are distinguished by their spires of pea-like flowers in white, blue, or mauve, or in combinations of these. Goat's rue (*G. officinalis*) makes a vigorous clump of rather lax stems bearing white, mauve, or bicolored flowers in a long season from early summer to early fall.

There are a number of cultivars, all growing to about 5ft (1.5m) tall. *G.* 'Candida' (formerly *G.* x *hartlandii* 'Candida') is a more erect plant than *G. officinalis* and bears spires of white flowers in long racemes. *G.* 'His Majesty' (syn. 'Her Majesty') has mauve and white flowers. *G.* 'Lady Wilson' has lilac and white flowers.

WHERE TO PLANT

Plant goat's rue in rich soil in sun or partial shade. It prefers moist soil, where it will spread quickly.

PLANT CARE

The more lax forms will need staking, and if you do not want the plants to self-seed, deadhead them after flowering. Sow seeds in a coldframe in spring; the seeds have a hard casing and may need soaking in order to improve germination. Alternatively, divide established plants in late autumn or early spring. Goat's rue is susceptible to pea and bean weevils but is otherwise trouble-free.

PLANTING SUGGESTIONS

Grow in a natural garden or wild meadow. The taller, more erect forms are useful cut flowers.

*The pea-like flowers of goat's rue (*Galega x hartlandii*) make a vivid display over a long period from summer to fall.*

Gunnera

GUNNERACEAE/HALORAGIDACEAE

Gunnera

Those of us familiar with the huge perennial giant rhubarb (*Gunnera manicata*) might be astonished to discover that, within this genus of about 45 species of herbaceous and evergreen perennials, there are some truly tiny species—*G. magellanica* (which has similarly shaped leaves) grows only 6in (15cm) high. However, giant rhubarb, which is native to South America, is the all-time garden giant, matched only by giant hogweed (*Heracleum mantegazzianum*), which cannot, in any case, be recommended for gardens. Giant rhubarb reaches a statuesque 8ft (2.5m) or more and can spread even more, to about 10ft (3m), with each individual leaf spanning some 5ft (1.5m).

Another species in this genus, *G. tinctoria* (syn. *G. chilensis*, *G. scabra*), is a large perennial, albeit smaller than *G. manicata*, reaching a mere 5ft (1.5m) in height with a spread of about 6ft (1.8m). Apart from size, it is similar to its cousin; indeed, the two are often easily confused in garden centers.

The colossal leaves of both species are rounded in overall shape, with several lobes and toothed edges. They have prominent veins and are a deep, rich, mid-green. The red-tinged stalks are covered in prickly bristles. Giant rhubarb flowers in summer, when the reddish-green flowers are borne in dense, conical, short-stemmed spires that are over 3ft (1m) long. Small reddish-green fruits follow the flowers.

WHERE TO PLANT

Grow the two large species in moist soil; in most gardens, this means creating a bog garden especially for it using a liner that is punctured in one or two places to increase the moisture-retaining qualities of the soil. Giant rhubarb also needs plenty of humus, but it will cope with either full sun or partial shade.

*Not a plant that is easy to ignore, giant rhubarb (*Gunnera manicata*) has leaves that span over 5ft (1.5m) in diameter.*

PLANT CARE

In colder areas, once the plant dies down, you should protect the vulnerable crowns by wrapping them with the faded leaves or by using a mulch of straw or burlap. You can grow giant rhubarb by collecting the seeds and sowing them in fall; keep them in a warm, light place. Germination may take some time. You can also propagate giant rhubarb by taking cuttings of the basal buds in spring. Although they are generally fairly trouble-free, giant rhubarb can be susceptible to attacks from aphids and whitefly.

PLANTING SUGGESTIONS

These large species are excellent architectural plants, creating a dramatic focal point in a garden, where they are completely impossible to overlook. Because they need reliably moist soil, they are often planted in the damp soil near a natural pool.

Helenium

ASTERACEAE/COMPOSITAE

Sneezeweed

The genus *Helenium* contains annuals, biennials, and perennials that can be found in North and Central America in damp areas or at the edge of woodland. Sneezeweed (*H. autumnale*), which is native to North America, is the largest species. It has long, lance-shaped, toothed leaves and bright golden, daisylike flowers that turn downward as the brownish florets that form the central disc open. The sturdy, branched stems bear a multitude of flowers from late summer to mid-autumn.

There is a selection of similarly large hybrids, many of German or Dutch origin, of which some of the best known are *H.* 'Feuersiegel', which has orange-brown flowers with brownish centers; *H.* 'Goldrausch', which has larger golden flowers than the species, about 3in (8cm) in diameter; *H.* 'Rubinkuppel', which has rich, rusty red flowers; and *H.* 'Septemberfuchs', which has burnt-orange-colored flowers with brown centers.

WHERE TO PLANT

Sneezeweed does best in fertile, moist, well-drained soil in full sun.

PLANT CARE

Heleniums generally do not require support unless they are in exposed areas. If you deadhead regularly, you will lengthen the flowering season. Divide every couple of years to promote vigor. You can propagate species from seed sown in spring, while cultivars should be propagated from basal cuttings taken in winter. Be careful when you handle the plants, because the leaves can cause skin allergies. *Heleniums* can be troubled by leaf spot but are otherwise usually trouble-free.

PLANTING SUGGESTIONS

All the plants look good in large, natural drifts in damp areas of the garden or in a bee border. You can cut the flowers for the house, as well.

*'Moerheim Beauty' is one of the most popular cultivars of sneezeweed (*Helenium*), a large, summer-flowering perennial.*

Helianthus

ASTERACEAE/COMPOSITAE

Sunflower

This genus includes the annual sunflower, which, although not a perennial, grows readily from seed; its huge, yellow, sunray flowers need no introduction. There are also cultivars with russet, mahogany, and lemon flowers.

Among the big perennials in this group, purple-disk sunflower (*H. atrorubens*) grows to about 5ft (1.5m) tall. The flowers have golden, narrow petals around dark brown-red centers and dark green, ovate, toothed leaves. *H.* 'Monarch' is a vigorous form growing up to 6ft (1.8m) tall and bearing semi-double flowers with yellowish-brown centers in early to mid-autumn. Mountain sun-flower (*H.* x *laetiflorus*) grows up to 7ft (2.2m) tall.

Thinleaf sunflower (*H. decapetalus*), which will grow up to 5ft (1.5m) tall, bears the familiar golden flowers with yellow-brown centers about 3in (8cm) in diameter. *H. decapetalus* 'Triomphe de Gand' forms tight-growing clumps, up to 6ft (1.8m) tall, with broad, golden-yellow, semi-double flowers. *H.* x *multiflorus* 'Loddon Gold' grows up to 5ft (1.5m) high and bears golden-yellow, double flowerheads.

WHERE TO PLANT

Grow in well drained, neutral to alkaline soil in full sun. Some will cope with dry soil but will need full sun to flower well; thinleaf sunflower, mountain sunflower, and *H.* x *multiflorus*, however, prefer damp soil, as long as it is never waterlogged.

PLANT CARE

In fall, put a dressing of bulky organic manure over the crowns. Species can be propagated from seeds sown *in situ* in late spring, but cultivars are best propagated from basal root cuttings in early spring. Divide in spring or autumn. Often affected by mildew and susceptible to attack by slugs.

PLANTING SUGGESTIONS

These are ideal additions to a natural border or wildflower garden, where they will attract bees.

Sunflowers make a cheerful addition to any border, and are best grown in large drifts.

Heliopsis helianthoides

ASTERACEAE/COMPOSITAE

Oxeye

There are about a dozen species of perennials in this genus, and most of them are found in the open land of North America. They are similar to *Helianthus* in many respects, and they may be confused with sunflowers.

The lance-shaped, toothed leaves of oxeye (*Heliopsis helianthoides*) are mid-green and have prominent veins. The all-yellow, daisylike flowers are fertile, unlike those of the sunflower, and the flowers grow to about 3in (8cm) in diameter and bloom from late summer to mid-autumn.

There is a good range of cultivars in various sizes, the largest being *H. helianthoides* 'Mars', which has single yellow-orange flowers and grows to about 5ft (1.5m) tall. Smooth oxeye (*H. helianthoides* var. *scabra*) bears fewer flowers and is slightly smaller, but *H. h.* var. *scabra* 'Goldgefieder' (Golden Plume) is another tall and impressive plant, with double, yellow flowers with greenish centers.

WHERE TO PLANT

These daisylike plants will grow best in moist, fertile soil in full sun.

PLANT CARE

The bigger species may need some support, especially if they are in an exposed position. They are best divided every three years or so to maintain vigor, and you can propagate from the divisions. Alternatively, sow seeds or root basal cuttings in spring. Young plants are susceptible to slug damage.

PLANTING SUGGESTIONS

Plant the species and cultivars toward the back of a sunny border with other members of the daisy family, such as inula and giant daisy (*Leucanthemella*).

There are both double- and single-flowered oxeyes, all distinguished by their eye-catching bright yellow flowers.

Humulus lupulus

CANNABIDACEAE

Common hop

The hop, a vigorous, twining herbaceous perennial, originates in the northern temperate regions, where it grows in hedgerows and woodlands. The hops themselves, which are actually the female flowers, are best known for their use in brewing; in the garden, however, common hop (*Humulus lupulus*) is grown primarily for its attractive foliage which can be either golden or variegated. The large leaves, which may have three or five lobes and grow to be 6in (15cm) long, have serrated edges and are light green in color.

In the summer, the distinctively aromatic green flowers gradually turn pale golden-brown. Golden hop (*H. lupulus* 'Aureus') is grown for its fresh-looking, golden-yellow foliage.

A close cousin, variegated Japanese hop (*H. japonicus* 'Variegatus'), is similar but has mottled green leaves and is an annual.

WHERE TO PLANT

Common hop needs moist but well-drained soil and a position in sun or partial shade. Golden hop needs full sun to achieve the best leaf color. You will need to provide a sturdy support system around which the shoots can twine.

PLANT CARE

Propagate by taking softwood cuttings in spring or greenwood cuttings in summer. Hops are generally easy to grow but can fall prey to verticillium wilt.

PLANTING SUGGESTIONS

Hops are usually grown against a wall or fence to which a system of wires has been attached, or over a pergola or pillar. They are useful climbers for providing shade in summer but because the growth dies back in winter they allow all available light into the garden in winter.

*The golden hop (*Humulus lupulus *'Aureus') is a great choice for mixing with clematis, providing excellent foliage color over a long period.*

Inula

ASTERACEAE/COMPOSITAE

Inula

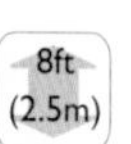

Inula magnifica, a big, sturdy plant and clump-forming herbaceous perennial, is one of many species in a genus that spans Africa and Asia in a broad cross-section of habitats. The daisylike flowers of *Inula magnifica* have narrow golden-yellow petals around a central boss or eye, also golden yellow. Each flower grows to about 6in (15cm) across and from late summer to mid-autumn, clusters of flowers are borne on branching stems. The leaves are long and dark green, and hairy on the undersides.

Among the other species in the genus, elecampane (*I. helenium*) is as large as *I. magnifica* at 5ft (1.5m). It has smaller flowerheads that only grow about 3in (8cm) across, but these are also bright yellow. The leaves, which have woolly undersides, grow up to 32in (80cm) long.

I. racemosa is even larger, growing to about 8ft (2.5m) tall and forming clumps up to 5ft (1.5m) across. The yellow flowers, however, are smaller, at about 2in (5–6cm) across, and the leaves are mid-green, large at the base, and becoming progressively smaller up the reddish stems.

WHERE TO PLANT

Inulas prefer moist but well-drained soil in sun, although elecampane will cope with partial shade and *I. magnifica* can be grown in a bog garden.

PLANT CARE

The tough, sturdy stems do not usually require staking. Sow seeds in spring or autumn, or you can divide clumps at this time also. Inulas are susceptible to powdery mildew in overly dry conditions but are otherwise trouble-free.

PLANTING SUGGESTIONS

These big species are good subjects for naturalized drifts. Elecampane is widely used for medicinal purposes (as an expectorant) and can therefore be included in an herb garden.

The large, multi-petaled heads of inula (Inula magnifica).

Iris

IRIDACEAE

Iris

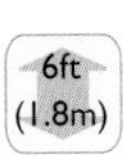

Of this hugely popular genus of rhizomatous or bulbous perennials, only a handful may be categorized as "giants." Irises are divided into different groups: bearded, in which the flowers have the familiar form of three raised upper petals (standards) and three drooping lower petals (falls); beardless, in which the standards are more horizontal and the falls droop less; and crested, which are similar to beardless but with wavy-edged petals. Of these, the two largest are the beardless Siberian irises and the Spuria irises, although a few of the water irises (*Laevigatae*) can grow to over 5ft (1.5m).

Siberian iris (*Iris sibirica*), from Russia and central and eastern Europe, is a rhizomatous beardless iris with long, grassy leaves. The flower stem rises high above the leaves in summer, bearing up to five bluish mauve upper petals, while the lower ones have darker veining and white markings.

WHERE TO PLANT

Laevigata irises need to be grown in shallow water or reliably moist, slightly acid soil. Siberian and Spuria irises prefer neutral to alkaline soil, but the soil must be reliably moist. All need full sun.

PLANT CARE

All beardless rhizomatous irises should be planted with the rhizomes below the soil surface, about 16in (40cm) apart. Mulch well after planting, but avoid high-nitrogen feeds, which can cause the rhizomes to rot. To encourage vigor divide every few years and use the divisions for propagation, making sure that each piece of rhizome has a new shoot bud. Beardless irises tend to suffer from gray mold and thrips.

PLANTING SUGGESTIONS

Plant Siberian and *Spuria* irises in a border. Plant *Laevigatae* irises at the margins of a pond.

Japanese irises are distinguished by their slightly flattened shape.

Kniphofia

ASPHODELACEAE/LILIACEAE

Torch lily, Poker plant, Red-hot-poker

Z 3–9

5ft (1.5m)

3ft (1m)

These striking plants—some evergreen, some deciduous—originate in southern Africa, but many are surprisingly hardy. The names torch lily and red-hot-poker derive from the eye-catching display of fiery-looking flowers produced by some species. The tubular or cylindrical flowers are packed into dense spires 16in (40cm) long. The leaves, which are generally arching and strap-shaped, can be long—to 5ft (1.5m) in the case of the evergreen *K. northiae*—and are bluish-green in color.

There are several large species and a few big hybrids. From early to late summer, *K. northiae* has spires of pale yellow flowers as well as exceptionally long, grassy leaves; the flowers grow up to 5ft (1.5m) tall and open from bright red buds. *K. uvaria* 'Nobilis', another evergreen plant, has long spires, up to 5ft (1.5m) tall, of deep orange-red flowers over a long period from midsummer to early autumn.

Of the many popular hybrids, the following are all about 5ft (1.5m) tall: K. 'Green Jade' has evergreen leaves and from late summer to early autumn bears greenish flowers that turn white; K. 'Ice Queen', another evergreen, has flowers that open from green buds to pale yellow and then fade to ivory from early to mid-autumn. K. 'Samuel's Sensation' is herbaceous and in late summer and early autumn bears scarlet flowers that turn yellowish as they fade. The biggest hybrid is K. 'Prince Igor', a herbaceous perennial whose glowing orange-red flowers stand out in late summer to early autumn.

WHERE TO PLANT

Torch lilies prefer sandy soil in full sun or partial shade, but they need plenty of organic matter incorporated in the soil to do well; the plants will need to be mulched with straw in cold winter areas, particularly when they are young. They need plenty of moisture, but the soil must be well-drained or the crowns may rot.

PLANT CARE

The easiest way to propagate torch lilies is by separating offshoots from the parent plant or by transplanting new shoots as basal cuttings. You can sow seeds in spring, but cultivars do not generally come true from seed. A more reliable way is to divide established clumps in spring. Torch lilies can suffer from thrips, evidence of which can be seen in mottled foliage. Violet root rot can also cause problems.

PLANTING SUGGESTIONS

These make a good central feature in an island bed, or they can be planted with other hot-colored perennials, in shades of gold, orange, and red such as *rudbeckia* and *helianthemum*.

*Above: The aptly named torch lily (*Kniphofia*) has brilliantly colored spires of flowers.*

Opposite: A mixed planting of species (red) and hybrid (red and yellow 'Royal Standard') kniphofias.

Lathyrus

LEGUMINOSAE/PAPILIONACEAE

Vetchling, Wild pea

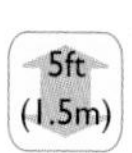

There are a number of species of perennials—some herbaceous, some evergreen—in this family. They all have the pea-like flowers that are typical of the family, and many are both scented and spectacular and bearing many flowers on each plant. Those that can be classed as giant are all climbers, using tendrils to cling to supports. Everlasting pea (*L. grandiflorus*) is an herbaceous perennial climber with clusters of up to four fairly small, pinkish red flowers about 1 in (3cm) long. Originating from southern Europe, it grows to about 5ft (1.5m) high.

Perennial pea, also called everlasting pea, (*L. latifolius*) is another herbaceous perennial, with clusters of smallish purplish-pink flowers from summer to early autumn. Cultivars include 'Blushing Bride', with apple-blossom-colored flowers, and 'White Pearl', with pure white blooms. The familiar sweet pea (*L. odoratus*) is an annual that can be grown as a biennial in zones 6–9 with many highly scented, colored and bicolored cultivars.

WHERE TO PLANT

Grow all everlasting peas in well-drained soil to which plenty of organic matter has been added, in full sun or dappled shade. They can also be grown in containers.

PLANT CARE

For a good display of flowers, feed with seaweed-based fertilizer every two weeks throughout the growing season, and deadhead regularly. Provide support in the form of a wigwam, trellis or horizontal wires. Propagate plants by chipping or soaking the seeds before sowing them *in situ* in mild areas or in a coldframe in colder areas in spring. Can be susceptible to a number of viruses and to attacks from slugs, snails, aphids and thrips.

PLANTING SUGGESTIONS

Grow over a hazel or willow tepee or in a border.

This sweet pea (Lathyrus odoratus) is supported by a traditional wigwam of hazel rods.

Lespedeza thunbergii

PAPILIONACEAE/LEGUMINOSAE

Thunberg bush clover

This subshrub hails from China and Japan, but it is best treated as an herbaceous perennial in cold climates.

There are forty species in the genus, but Thunberg bush clover (*Lespedeza thunbergii*) is the only one commonly grown in gardens. It is cultivated for its long, delicate arching shoots which bear small, pea-like, purplish-pink flowers. The flowers densely cover the last 6in (15cm) of the stems in autumn. Because it flowers at a time of year when there are fewer flowers to choose from, this is a valuable addition to any border. The mid-green leaves have three distinct leaflets; this feature has given rise to the common name of bush clover.

WHERE TO PLANT

Bush clover prefers well-drained, light soil and a position in full sun.

PLANT CARE

After flowering, cut plants down to ground level. Propagate from seeds sown in spring or from greenwood cuttings taken in early summer. You can also propagate bush clover from divisions in early spring. Treat bush clover as a perennial in cold areas, cutting it to ground level in autumn (no staking). There are no known pests and diseases.

PLANTING SUGGESTIONS

This plant looks good against a wall at the back of a border or in a mixed shrub and perennial border.

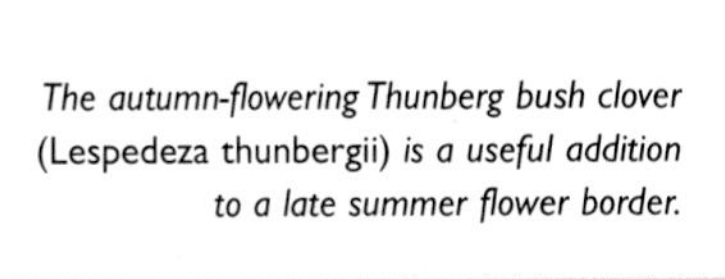

The autumn-flowering Thunberg bush clover (Lespedeza thunbergii) *is a useful addition to a late summer flower border.*

Leucanthemella serotina

COMPOSITAE

High daisy, Giant daisy

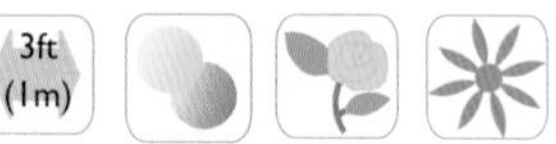

Formerly known as *Chrysanthemum serotinum* or *C. uliginosum*, high daisy (*Leucanthemella serotina*) is a tough, herbaceous perennial that looks much like the oxeye daisy (*Chrysanthemum Leucanthemum*). It can be found growing wild in the marshlands of southern Europe and eastern Asia. It has larger flowerheads, about 3in (8cm) across, than its cousin, and each is composed of many small narrow, white petals with a central raised, greenish-yellow boss of stamens. The flowers are carried either singly on the stems or in loose clusters of up to eight flowerheads. The stems are hairy and the leaves are long, fairly narrow and lance-shaped with sharply toothed edges. They are borne alternately up the stem of the plant.

WHERE TO PLANT

Grow in any sunny or partially shaded site in moisture-retentive soil.

PLANT CARE

A tough, vigorous plant, high daisy will survive with remarkably little attention, although clumps will need to be divided in spring every two or three years. You can propagate it from basal cuttings taken in spring or by division. Young plants are susceptible to slug damage, and thrips can be a problem.

PLANTING SUGGESTIONS

Grow the species in a damp mixed or herbaceous border or in a bog garden. It will do well with other marshland plants, such as coneflowers (*Rudbeckia*), astilbes (*Astilbe*) and leopard plants (*Ligularia*).

*The giant daisy (*Leucanthemella serotina*), which enjoys damp soil, is a hardy plant.*

Ligularia

ASTERACEAE/COMPOSITAE

Leopard plant

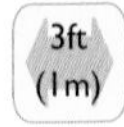

This genus includes some of the most deserving of the giant perennials, offering both handsome foliage and striking flowerheads in shades of yellow, orange and rust. They demand a damp site and are ideal for boggy patches of the garden.

There are several species and a few hybrids to choose from, all big … and some even bigger! Among the biggest is *Ligularia przewalskii* (syn. *Senecio przewalskii*), which grows up to 6ft (1.8m) tall. It forms clumps of handsome large leaves, up to 12in (30cm) long, cut in a filigree fashion, with irregularly shaped lobes and serrated edges. The flowers form tall spires of delicate orange-yellow blooms on dark stems in mid- and late summer.

L. stenocephala, which grows up to 5ft (1.5m) tall, has triangularly pointed leaves with heart-shaped bases, up to 14in (35cm) long, and in early and late summer it bears spires of yellow flowers with orange yellow centers on darkish stems. Its hybrid with *L. przewalskii*, *L.* 'The Rocket' is bigger, up to 6ft (1.8m) tall, and has dramatic black stems. Also large is *L.* x *hessei* 'Gregynog Gold', which has even bigger leaves and flowers than *L. przewalskii*. The daisylike, orange-yellow flowers are about 4in (10cm) across and are borne in conical flowerheads.

WHERE TO PLANT

They need fairly rich soil that never dries out, and protection from cold winds, with some shade.

PLANT CARE

Tough plants, these have few needs other than adequate moisture, good soil fertility, and some midday shade. You can sow seeds *in situ* in spring or divide clumps of established plants after flowering. The young shoots and leaves may be attacked by slugs and snails, but otherwise they are trouble-free.

PLANTING SUGGESTIONS

Plant leopard plants in big drifts.

*Leopard plants (*Ligularia*) are ideal for bog gardens.* Ligularia 'The Rocket' *produces strikingly tall spires of flowers on dark stems.*

Lilium

LILIACEAE

Lily

Lilies are among the most sumptuous of herbaceous perennials, with their striking, large, waxy flowers, many of them scented, which grow from bulbs with overlapping, fleshy scales. Many hybrids and some species attain giant proportions. Lilies are divided into nine different categories, according to their characteristics, and the flowers are either trumpet-shaped, bowl-shaped, turk's cap (with reflexed petals), or funnel-shaped.

One of the most familiar lilies is king lily (*Lilium regale*), which comes from China. It grows up to 6ft (1.8m) tall with up to 25 trumpet-shaped, white flowers with the most exquisite scent in midsummer. The flowers are flushed purple on the outside with yellow centers and bright yellow anthers. The leaves are long and strappy.

American Turk's cap lily (*L. superbum*) is a true giant, growing up to 10ft (3m) tall. The leaves grow in dense whorls, and the slightly drooping flowers, orange with maroon spots, appear in late summer and early autumn.

Leopard lily (*L. pardalinum*), another American lily, is similar, with reflexed, bright orange, maroon-spotted flowers in midsummer.

Madonna lily (*L. candidum*) grows up to 6ft (1.8m) tall and bears pure white, trumpet-shaped, scented flowers that have bright yellow antlers. Unlike other lilies, the base leaves remain throughout the winter.

WHERE TO PLANT

Lilies prefer moist, well-drained soil, and many prefer slightly acid soil, although there are some species, including madonna lily, that either prefer alkaline soil or are tolerant of it. Most will do best in full sun but will tolerate some shade.

Left: Lilium candidum *is a striking plant with richly scented white flowers.*

PLANT CARE

Plant lily bulbs two and a half times their own depth in autumn; those that are stem-rooting need to be planted even deeper, but plant madonna lily close to the soil surface. Once the lilies are growing, feed with a high-potassium fertilizer once every two weeks until they flower. Propagate from offsets (small scales or bulbs attached to the parent bulb), which can be removed and planted up in late summer.

Lilies are susceptible to attacks by lily beetle, which are quite easily spotted and can be removed by hand. They can also be troubled by aphids, thrips, leatherjackets, and wireworms, and by a number of viruses, although some cultivars that are virus-resistant have been developed.

PLANTING SUGGESTIONS

Plant the tall species lilies at the back of herbaceous borders or in large containers. Some of the hybrids are not quite as tall, and these are ideal for containers that can be moved around to fill gaps in a summer scheme. Hybrids in the Golden Splendor Group, for example, have large, showy, golden, scented, bowl-shaped flowers with maroon stripes, and *L.* 'Black Beauty' has scented dark red turk's cap flowers.

Lilium bulbiferum *is vigorous but unscented.*

Macleaya

PAPAVERACEAE

Plume poppy

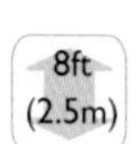

These rhizomatous perennials are grown primarily for their foliage and secondarily for their flowers. Plume poppy (*Macleaya cordata*) has leaves with five to seven lobes and large, delicate spires of creamy white flowers in mid- to late summer. *M. microcarpa* 'Kelway's Coral Plume', which is slightly smaller at 7ft (2.2m) tall, has coral pink flowers that open from pink buds from early summer. *M.* x *kewensis* 'Flamingo', which grows up to 8ft (2.5m) tall, also has pink buds and pinkish-buff flowers.

WHERE TO PLANT

Plume poppies are tolerant plants that grow well in most soils and positions, including partial shade. Ideally, they prefer fairly rich, moist, well-drained soil. Protect them from cold, drying winds.

PLANT CARE

The erect, slightly glaucous stems do not require staking. You can propagate from self-sown seedlings, from rooted rhizomes during the plant's dormancy, from seeds sown in spring, or from root cuttings taken in winter; however, because the plants self-seed freely, propagation may not be an issue! Little seems to damage them, although slugs can attack young seedlings.

PLANTING SUGGESTIONS

Plume poppies are perfect plants for a semi-wild border. Alternatively, they work very well as a tall screen or at the back of the border.

Macleaya x kewensis *is a statuesque foliage plant with huge, grayish-green leaves.*

Matteuccia struthiopteris

DRYOPTERIDACEAE/WOODSIACEAE

Ostrich fern

These deciduous terrestrial ferns occur naturally in the woodlands of Europe, eastern Asia, and North America. They produce a distinctive plume of upright, broadly lance-shaped, typical ferny fronds, with slender leaflets arranged alternately up the main stem.

A secondary flush of fronds appears in late summer inside the main plume of fronds, which is shorter and darkish-brown in color. This fern is rhizomatous, and in the right conditions the rhizomes will spread, sending up separate small plumes.

WHERE TO PLANT

Like most ferns, these will do best in a shady border or in partial shade near a pond or stream, in moist, humus-rich, well-drained, neutral or slightly acidic soil.

PLANT CARE

Ferns are more or less maintenance free, but give them an annual dressing of seaweed-based fertilizer. Propagate by detaching any new plumes that arise in early spring or sow the spores (which can be found on the undersides of the fronds) in warmth in autumn. Ferns do not get damaged by pests and diseases.

PLANTING SUGGESTIONS

Grow in a small, shady border, in a woodland garden, or at the margins of an informal pool for best effect.

*The handsome ostrich fern (*Matteuccia struthiopteris*) does best in damp, shady borders.*

Meconopsis

PAPAVERACEAE

Himalayan blue poppy

There are several deciduous or evergreen perennials in this genus, originating in mountainous, moist, shady areas in India, Tibet and China; of these, Tibetan poppy (*Meconopsis grandis*) is one of the most familiar. Although not truly a giant at 5ft (1.5m) tall, this is nonetheless a large, handsome poppy, all the more distinguished for its rich blue, cup-shaped flowers with prominent yellow stamens in early summer. The flowers, up to 6in (15cm) in diameter and borne singly on long stalks, nod slightly. Originating in Nepal and Tibet, this is a clump-forming, deciduous perennial with longish leaves that are toothed at the edges and borne in a basal rosette; on the stems, a whorl of leaves is set just below the flowers. These are darker green and covered in reddish-brown hairs.

Larger, at 8ft (2.5m) high, but less commonly grown, is Himalayan poppy (*M. napaulensis*). It has branching stems bearing pink, red or purple poppy-like flowers, up to 3in (8cm) across, from late spring to midsummer.

WHERE TO PLANT

These species need moist but well-drained, humus-rich, slightly acid soil and a position in partial shade, sheltered from cold, drying winds. They do best in climates with cool, wet summers.

PLANT CARE

Make sure that the soil has plenty of leaf mold added to it, so that it is both humus-rich and drains well. Create a shelter belt from cold, prevailing winds. Sow the seeds in a coldframe in autumn or spring, but make sure that the seedlings are kept moist and in good light. Autumn seedlings should be overwintered in a cold greenhouse or a coldframe. Slugs and snails attack young seedlings, and more mature plants are susceptible to downy mildew.

PLANTING SUGGESTIONS

These imposing poppies should be grown in a shady border or in a woodland garden.

The Himalayan blue poppy (Meconopsis)*—this one belongs to the George Sherriff Group—has unusual large, blue flowers.*

Melianthus major

MELIANTHACEAE

Honey bush

The species is classified as a shrub, but it can be treated as a perennial in climates where the temperature does not fall far below 23°F (–5°C), because the plant will normally regrow from the base. It originates from the Cape in South Africa.

Honey bush is the architectural plant *par excellence*. The leaves, which have an almost pleated appearance, are some 20in (50cm) long. They are blue-gray-green in color with up to 17 sharply toothed, slightly folded leaflets per leaf. In late spring, long spikes of brick red flowers are borne.

WHERE TO PLANT

Honey bush needs to be planted in full sun in well-drained, reasonably fertile soil.

PLANT CARE

The stems are sturdy, so no staking is needed. Mulch around the base of the plant in winter with straw or organic matter, and make sure that the plant does not become waterlogged. Provide shelter from cold, drying winds. If you plant it as a container plant, you can overwinter it indoors in particularly cold weather.

PLANTING SUGGESTIONS

As a foliage feature, plant honey bush on a terrace, for example, or in pots. It does well in seaside gardens, coming as it does from coastal regions of South Africa.

*Honey flower (*Melianthus major*) has curiously pleated leaves and will withstand seaside conditions.*

Miscanthus

GRAMINEAE/POACEAE

Silver grass, Eulalia grass

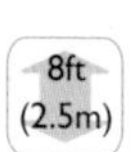

Grasses have increased in popularity, and there are several species of silvergrass that are worth including in an herbaceous border or as an architectural foliage plant. Silver grasses occur naturally in marshlands in Africa and eastern Asia. Some species and cultivars grow particularly tall. Giant Chinese silver grass (*Miscanthus floridulus*) can reach up to 8ft (2.5m). It has the typical arching slender leaves of the genus, up to 3ft (1m) long, and upright, spiky, silvery flowerheads.

The more commonly grown Japanese silver grass (*M. sinensis*) (or eulalia grass) has long, arching, blue-green leaves and purplish spikes of flowers in autumn. There are numerous cultivars, still large, but smaller than *M. sinensis* 'Silberfeder' (Silver feather), which grows up to 8ft (2.5m) and is distinguished by its pinkish-brown flower panicles in autumn; these persist throughout the winter. *M. sinensis* subsp. *condensatus* 'Cabaret' is grown for its distinctive foliage: the broad, mid-green leaves have bold white stripes; it grows up to 6ft (1.8m) tall. Equally distinctively marked is *M. sinensis* 'Variegatus', also up to 6ft (1.8m); the leaves have lengthwise green and white stripes.

WHERE TO PLANT

These grasses do best in moist soil in full sun. Make sure that the soil around the roots does not become waterlogged in winter.

PLANT CARE

Leave the flowerheads uncut for winter color, but cut the plants down to ground level in early spring to improve vigor. Pot up divisions in spring. These may take a while to establish, however. Silver grass is not normally troubled by pests and diseases.

PLANTING SUGGESTIONS

Grow these grasses as an architectural feature plant in a container or as part of a flowering border.

*An elegant grass, Japanese silver grass (*Miscanthus sinensis* 'Silberfeder') has attractive silvery-brown flower heads.*

Molinia caerulea

GRAMINEAE/POACEAE

Purple moor grass

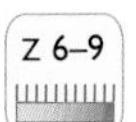

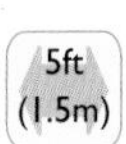

This densely tufted perennial grass is native to the damp marshlands of Europe and parts of Asia. Purple moor grass (*Molinia caerulea*) is grown primarily for its attractive, upright yellow stems, which bear purple-brown flower spikes for a long season from spring to autumn. The long, narrow leaves form a dense clump at the base and are mid-green with a purple base.

M. caerulea subsp. *arundinacea* 'Karl Foerster' has longer leaves than the species, about 3ft (1m), and purple flower spikes on delicately arching stems. It grows to about 4ft (1.2m) tall. The aptly named *M. c.* subsp. *arundinacea* 'Skyracer' towers over it at 8ft (2.5m). The leaves turn gold in autumn.

WHERE TO PLANT

Moor grass will grow in most situations, in sun or partial shade, but it prefers neutral to acid soil.

PLANT CARE

These grasses are easy to grow and have no special needs. Propagate species only by sowing seeds in spring; established plants of cultivars can be divided in spring. There are no pests and diseases to worry about.

PLANTING SUGGESTIONS

These grasses can be grown in a mixed or herbaceous border or in a container. Grow with other grasses, or with purple flowered perennials, such as bee balm (*Monarda*). They are also useful in woodland gardens.

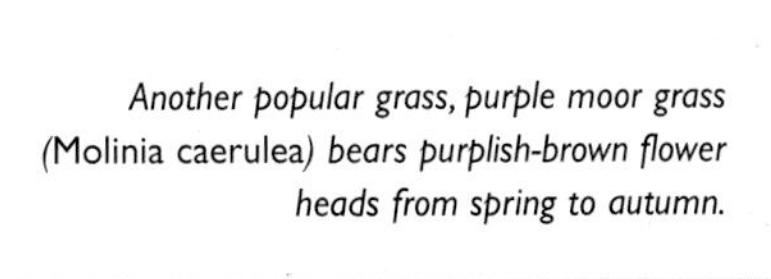

*Another popular grass, purple moor grass (*Molinia caerulea*) bears purplish-brown flower heads from spring to autumn.*

Monarda

LABIATAE/LAMIACEAE

Bee balm, Bergamot

There are 12 species of annuals and rhizomatous herbaceous perennials in this genus, but the only two that are "giants" are *M.* 'Comanche', which reaches 6ft (1.8m) and has mid-pink flowers, and *M.* 'Mohawk', which, at 5ft (1.5m), is slightly smaller and has deep lilac-mauve flowers with dark bracts. Both flower from midsummer to early autumn.

WHERE TO PLANT

Grow bee balm in full sun or light shade in moist, well-drained soil.

PLANT CARE

Although relatively easy to grow, bee balm is prey to mildew. Slugs and snails can also cause damage. You need to make sure that the plants do not get waterlogged in winter or dry out in summer. Sow seeds in spring or autumn or divide clumps in early spring. You can also propagate from basal cuttings in spring.

PLANTING SUGGESTIONS

Use bee balm for added autumn and winter interest in an herbaceous border.

*The purplish-pink flowers of bee balm (*Monarda*) are excellent candidates for the late summer border.*

Musa basjoo

MUSACEAE

Japanese banana

Ideal for growing in large containers in colder climates, Japanese banana (*Musa basjoo*, syn. *M. japonica*) is a wonderfully architectural foliage plant with huge, paddle-shaped, visibly veined leaves in soft apple green, slightly folded at the edges. The leaves can reach 10ft (3m) in length. In summer, smallish, pale yellow flowers with large brown bracts appear in drooping flower spikes. These may be followed by the fruit. The tiny, orange-yellow bananas are, unfortunately, inedible and contain black seeds in the white pulp.

WHERE TO PLANT

The Japanese banana plant is best grown in containers in all but the hottest climates, where it can be grown in a sheltered spot in full sun. Site the plants away from the wind, which quickly damages the leaves, tearing them and turning them brown at the edges. In a greenhouse or conservatory, grow it in a large container with good quality compost and in good light.

PLANT CARE

In the growing season, feed with a seaweed-based fertilizer once every few weeks and keep well watered. In winter, keep the compost just moist. Overwinter indoors under glass in colder climates, or wrap the pots in layers of bubblewrap in areas with light frosts. Repot containers every couple of years to maintain vigor. Propagate from suckers. Aphids and mealybugs can be problems.

PLANTING SUGGESTIONS

Grow these large plants in containers on a terrace or patio.

*The Japanese banana (*Musa basjoo*) has striking, paddle-shaped leaves; it needs winter protection.*

Myrrhis odorata

APIACEAE/UMBELLIFERAE

Sweet cicely, anise

An aromatic, herbaceous perennial, sweet cicely (*Myrrhis odorata*) comes from mountainous areas of southern Europe and parts of Asia. The leaves are particularly pretty—fern-like, delicate, and bright green in color. The flowers, which are small, star-shaped, and pure white, appear in clusters in early summer, and are followed by small, shiny brown fruits.

The young shoots and leaves are used to add sweetness to stewed fruit (they are low in calories for those on diets), and the seeds have an aniseed-like flavor and are often added to salads or bread.

WHERE TO PLANT

Grow sweet cicely in dappled shade in moist but well-drained soil.

PLANT CARE

Add plenty of organic matter to the soil at planting time. If you are using the leaves for culinary purposes, remove the flowering stems as they develop; this will improve the flavor of the leaves. Plants need little attention otherwise and are free from pests and diseases. They self-seed freely, so propagation is not a problem, but you can sow seeds in spring or autumn or when they are ripe and divide plants in spring or autumn.

PLANTING SUGGESTIONS

Grow sweet cicely in a mixed border or in an herb garden, with some other large imposing herbs such as bergamot (*Monarda*) and common fennel (*Ferula communis*).

*Anise (*Myrrhis odorata*) is a tall herb that does best in moist shade. Grow it for its handsome foliage.*

Oenothera

ONAGRACEAE

Evening primrose

There are annuals, biennials, and perennials in the genus, but probably the best-known member is common evening primrose (*Oenothera biennis*), a biennial whose seeds are used to produce evening primrose oil—a much-valued natural remedy for premenstrual tension. It is a handsome plant with large, lance-shaped, lightly toothed leaves, up to 6in (15cm) long, in rosette formation. The flowers, borne for a long season from summer to autumn, are eye-catching: bright yellow and fragrant, they are bowl-shaped and up to 2in (5cm) across. They are notable for opening in the evening, hence the common name.

Red-sepal evening primrose (*O. glazioviana*), which originates from North America, is similar in most respects but has even longer leaves and larger flowers.

WHERE TO PLANT

Evening primroses do best in moderately poor, moisture-retentive soil in full sun.

PLANT CARE

Evening primroses do not normally require staking. They will self-seed freely in the right conditions, or you can sow them in early autumn to propagate them if they do not self-seed. They are susceptible to damage by slugs and can be troubled by mildews and leaf spot. Rot may occur if the conditions are too wet for them.

PLANTING SUGGESTIONS

Evening primroses can be planted in a sunny mixed border or, because they are attractive to butterflies, in a wild garden.

*The evening primrose (*Oenothera*) is another popular herb, with fragrant, cup-shaped yellow flowers.*

Onopordum

ASTERACEAE/COMPOSITAE

Cotton thistle, Scotch thistle

Scotch thistle (*Onopordum acanthium*) is a real whopper, growing up to 10ft (3m) tall and 3ft (1m) across. It is a rosette-forming biennial. The big, spiny, gray-green leaves are covered in soft gray hairs in the first year; in summer of the second year, massive branching, white, woolly stems bear ball-shaped, spine-tipped, thistle-like purple or white flowerheads.

O. nervosum is similar, but it grows up to 8ft (2.5m) tall and about 3ft (1m) across. It has even bigger leaves, up to 20in (50cm) long, and bright purplish-red-topped thistles, which are also borne in summer.

WHERE TO PLANT

Scotch thistles will do well in a gravel garden, and they generally prefer well-drained, slightly alkaline, light soil and a sunny, sheltered position.

PLANT CARE

These imposing plants require little maintenance, although slugs and snails can damage the young foliage. Propagate from seeds sown *in situ* in autumn or spring or transplant self-sown seedlings. Like all thistles, scotch thistles self-seed freely (sometimes too freely).

PLANTING SUGGESTIONS

Grow these as a feature plant, at the back of a border, or as the central feature in an island bed with other tall sun-loving perennials, such as mulleins (*Verbascum*) and foxtail lilies (*Eremurus*). The flowers are attractive to bees, so scotch thistle is often grown in a wildlife garden.

*The cotton thistle (*Onopordum*) is a candidate for the back of the border, where its metallic, gray-green leaves catch the light.*

Ostrowskia magnifica

CAMPANULACEAE

Giant bellflower

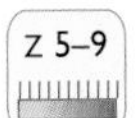

Originating on hillsides in Asia, this giant member of the campanula family has seven-petalled, bell-shaped flowers, in shades of light- to mid-blue, with a purple-striped throat and golden stamens, from early- to midsummer. Plants form upright clumps with narrow, oval and toothed leaves.

WHERE TO PLANT

Grow in full sun in deep soil with moist but fertile soil that is free-draining.

PLANT CARE

You may need to protect young shoots from late frosts with a mulch, but they are otherwise hardy. Avoid wet conditions when the plant is dormant. Staking may be helpful in exposed positions. The giant bellflower is not particularly easy to propagate, because the seedlings will not produce flowers in the first couple of years, and root cuttings, which should be taken in autumn, can be difficult to get established. The young shoots are attractive to slugs and snails.

PLANTING SUGGESTIONS

Grow in a sunny blue border alongside bog sage (*Salvia uliginosa*), Italian bugloss (*Anchusa azurea* 'Loddon Royalist'), and Russian sage (*Perovskia* 'Blue Spire').

The bell-shaped flowers of Ostrowskia magnifica.

Persicaria polymorpha

POLYGONACEAE

Knotweed

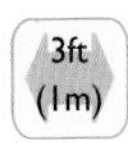

There are many annuals and perennials, and a few subshrubs in this genus, and they are widely distributed across the world. The perennials are either rhizomatous or stoloniferous; as a result of this, they spread quickly—sometimes becoming invasive—but making good groundcover as a consequence. They are ideally suited to meadow or woodland gardens.

There is one giant, knotweed (*Polygonum polymorpha*), which grows to a statuesque 8ft (2.5m) with creamy white plumes of flowers from midsummer to autumn. Unlike many of its cousins, it is not invasive but instead forms a tight clump, making it an ideal subject as a specimen plant.

WHERE TO PLANT

Grow in moist soil in full sun or partial shade.

PLANT CARE

This is an easy-to-maintain plant that needs no staking. Divide the clumps in spring or autumn to maintain vigor and to establish new plants, or sow seeds in a coldframe in spring. They can occasionally attract blackfly, and slugs and snails may damage young shoots. Be careful when handling the plants, because contact with any part may irritate the skin (and the sap can cause mild stomach aches).

PLANTING SUGGESTIONS

Grow this large perennial in a woodland garden or as part of a perennial border, where it should be planted in natural drifts. It combines well with other members of the genus, such as snakeweed (*P. bistorta* 'Superba'), which is smaller, to 4ft (1.2m), and bears dense spikes of pink flowers on dark stems from summer through to autumn. A semi-evergreen plant, it has long, visibly veined, mid-green leaves and will cope with drier soil than smartweed.

*Above: Smaller species, such as jumpseed (*Persicaria virginiana*), grow to around 4ft (1.2m).*
*Left: The biggest smartweed (*Persicaria polymorpha*) grows to 8ft (2.5m).*

Polygonatum

CONVALLARIACEAE/LILIACEAE

Solomon's seal

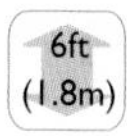

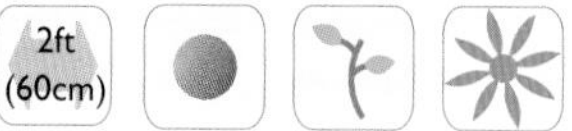

A rhizomatous perennial, Solomon's seal (*Polygonatum biflorum*, syn. *P. commutatum*, *P. giganteum*) can be found in woodland areas of Europe and North America. It has attractive foliage, the long, slightly pleated-looking, mid-green leaves borne alternately along the arching stems and having a slightly waxy appearance. The greenish-white flowers are tubular or bell-shaped, usually in clusters dangling from the lower sides of the stems and borne between the leaf stalks and the main stem. Flowering is from late spring to midsummer. After flowering, small round black fruit appear.

The hybrid *P.* x *hybridum* (a cross between *P. multiflorum* and *P. odoratum*) is similar but grows about 5ft (1.5m) tall and 1ft (30cm) across. The leaves are slightly longer and held horizontally. The greenish-white flowers are carried in clusters of four at each leaf joint and appear in late spring. They are followed by small, bluish-black, round fruit.

WHERE TO PLANT

Solomon's seal does well in a shady position in moist, well-drained, fertile soil, although it will also cope with full sun.

PLANT CARE

Solomon's seal is easy to care for and needs no staking. It will benefit from a dressing of organic matter in spring. Propagate from seed in autumn or divide the rhizomes in early spring. The young shoots are vulnerable to slug damage, and sawfly larvae can also be a problem.

PLANTING SUGGESTIONS

This is just the plant for a natural woodland garden or any shady part of the garden. The attractive foliage gives it a long season of appeal.

The small, bell-shaped flowers of Solomon's seal dangle from the arching stems.

Primula florindae

PRIMULACEAE

Tibetan cowslip

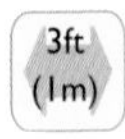

Although not technically a giant, Tibetan cowslip (*Primula florindae*) is by far the biggest species in this genus of otherwise fairly small herbaceous perennials. As its name suggests, Tibetan cowslip is native to the banks and borders of streams in southeast Tibet. The leaves form the typical primula rosettes, but are really big, up to 18in (45cm) long. They are mid-green with a prominent central vein and slightly wavy margins. The flowers form at the tip of the long, surprisingly robust-looking stems and droop delicately with as many as 40 individual flowers in a cluster. Bright yellow in color, they are funnel-shaped and fragrant.

WHERE TO PLANT

Grow Tibetan cowslips in full sun or in partial shade, in moist, humus-rich, slightly acid soil. In sunny positions the soil must be kept moist at all times.

PLANT CARE

The plants require little maintenance, but the soil must be moist all year-round, and it is important to add sufficient organic matter to it each year. They are susceptible to quite a wide range of problems, from the usual slugs and aphids to various rots and viruses. You can sow seeds in late winter or early spring. Alternatively, the plants can be divided between autumn and early spring, or you could take basal cuttings in autumn or early spring or root cuttings in winter.

PLANTING SUGGESTIONS

These are lovely in a bog garden or at the edges of a pond, particularly around one with a natural shape with sloping margins. They combine well with other bog plants, such as Japanese irises (*Iris japonica*), rodgersias (*Rodgersia*), astilbes (*Astilbe*) and hostas (*Hosta*).

*Although not strictly a giant, the Tibetan cowslip (*Primula florindae*) is the giant of its kind, with brilliantly colored, candelabra-like flowers.*

Rheum

POLYGONACEAE

Rhubarb

Although we are all familiar with edible rhubarb (*R.* x *hybridum*) in the vegetable garden, the ornamental versions certainly deserve a place in the flower garden. Chinese rhubarb (*Rheum palmatum*) is not at all dissimilar in appearance to its culinary cousin, having large, hand-shaped, toothed leaves with deeply marked veins, but it is an altogether more imposing plant. The leaves of Chinese rhubarb are truly huge, up to almost 3ft (1m) wide and long. They are purplish-red on their undersides and slightly hairy, and they emerge from large, bright red, conspicuous buds in spring. The flower stalk gives the plant its giant appearance, bearing plumes of creamy or bright pink flowers (according to the cultivar) in midsummer. *R. palmatum* 'Bowles' Crimson', for example, has bright crimson flowers and leaves that are noticeably red on the undersides. *R. palmatum* var. *tangutica* has plumes of white, pink or cream flowers. *R. palmatum* 'Atrosanguineum' (syn. 'Atropurpureum') has the best-looking foliage: the leaves are deep purplish-red when young, fading slowly to a dark green, and it has tall clusters of reddish-purple flowers, which can reach up to 8ft (2.5m) in height.

WHERE TO PLANT

Grow Chinese rhubarb in moist, fertile soil, in full sun or partial shade.

PLANT CARE

These plants need almost no attention, apart from ensuring that the soil stays moist. They are best planted in a bog garden, created with a butyl liner which has had a few holes punctured in the base so that moisture is retained, but the soil does not become waterlogged. A good dressing of organic matter in late autumn will help ensure a good crop of leaves the following spring. You can propagate from divisions in early spring, removing the new small crowns as they appear. Most ornamental rhubarbs are fairly trouble free, but look out for clusters of blackfly on the undersides of leaves early in the year. They can usually be removed by spraying the plant with water.

*Far right: The Chinese rhubarb (*Rheum palmatum*) does best in moist shade, where it will produce large clumps of magnificent hand-shaped leaves.*

PLANTING SUGGESTIONS

Plant in a bog garden or by the side of a stream or pond. Chinese rhubarb makes an impressive architectural feature, so make sure that it has enough space around it to be fully appreciated. Bamboos and Tibetan primulas, as well as ligularias and rodgersias, make good bog-garden bedfellows.

Above: The flower spike of Chinese rhubarb can grow to 8ft (2.2m) or more.

Rodgersia

SAXIFRAGACEAE

Rodgersia

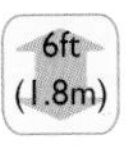

There are several noteworthy, tough, clump-forming perennials in this genus. They are all moisture-lovers, originating in the wet woodlands of Asia and Japan, where they are often found bordering streams. They are notable for their handsome foliage, which varies in shape from species to species, and in the summer they bear spires of star-shaped white or pink flowers in tall, fluffy-looking clusters. These are followed by darkish red or brown fruits.

Fingerleaf rodgersia (*R. aesculifolia*) has large leaves, up to 12in (30cm) long, which are similar to those of the horsechestnut. Each leaf is composed of up to nine leaflets and has a woolly red stalk and veins. The little starry flowers, in pink or white, are carried in tall, airy clusters in midsummer. Plants grow up to 6ft (1.8m) tall and 3ft (1m) across.

R. podophylla (syn. *R. japonica*) is shorter, at 5ft (1.5m) tall, but has a more spreading habit, to 6ft (1.8m). Its really big, hand-shaped leaves can grow up to 16in (40cm) long. They are quite different from those of fingerleaf rodgersia, each having up to five jagged lobes. Young leaves are bronze, but they turn green as they age, finally turning coppery-red in autumn. The greenish-white flowers are borne in sprays, up to 12in (30cm) long, in mid- to late summer.

Rodgersias are good all round plants, with both eye-catching foliage and attractive flowers.

WHERE TO PLANT

Rodgersias should be planted in moist, humus-rich soil in partial shade or full sun. They do not cope well with dry conditions, whether it is a lack of moisture in the soil or a cold, drying wind, but they will manage better in shade than in sun when conditions are less than perfect.

PLANT CARE

Rodgersias are sturdy enough to need no staking. Apply a good dressing of organic matter in early spring, which will also help to protect the young shoots from late frosts. Otherwise, these plants need little attention as long as they are kept well watered. Propagate from divisions in spring or sow seeds in a coldframe in spring. They are generally free from pests and diseases, although slugs may attack young shoots.

PLANTING SUGGESTIONS

Rodgersias will do best in a damp shady border, in a woodland garden, or in a bog garden, where they will associate well with Japanese primroses (*Primula japonica*), astilbes (*Astilbe*) and hostas (*Hosta*), all of which also have attractive foliage and like damp conditions. If you are prepared to do a lot of watering, you can grow them successfully in containers.

A slightly smaller, but equally handsome, form is *R. pinnata* 'Superba', which grows to about 4ft (1.2m) high with a spread of 40in (75cm). The leaves are heavily veined and a dark glossy green, borne in whorls of up to nine oval leaflets. The flowers are bright pink, and the foliage is beautifully tinged with bronze.

Romneya coulteri

PAPAVERACEAE

Matilija poppy, Tree poppy

This woody-based, shrubby perennial (sometimes classified as a subshrub) is found on scrubland in New Mexico. It spreads quickly by suckers. A star performer, it has large, poppy-like, cup-shaped, white flowers, each about 5in (12cm) across and with a prominent central boss of bright yellow stamens. The flowers are scented and are borne over a long period throughout summer. The waxy gray-green leaves are divided into three to five oval lobes.

There is a cultivar, *Romneya coulteri* 'White Cloud', which is particularly vigorous and spreading, with even more waxy leaves than the species.

WHERE TO PLANT

Matilija poppies need a sheltered position in full sun with fertile, well-drained soil. A sheltered, sunny border is ideal, but the vigorous, spreading suckers have been known to damage the fabric of nearby walls, so site the plants with care.

PLANT CARE

Matilija poppies can be difficult to establish because they resent transplanting; once they get underway, though, you may well be able to establish a sizeable colony as new plants emerge from suckers. They benefit from being mulched in the winter to protect the crowns. In colder climates frost will cut them back for you, but in milder areas they should be cut back to ground level in early spring.

PLANTING SUGGESTIONS

Matilija poppies associate well with other sun-loving plants, such as poppies (*Meconopsis*), columbines (*Aquilegia*), sage (*Salvia*) and ornamental onions (*Allium*).

*Matilija poppy (*Romneya coulteri*) has magnificent, large, white, poppy-like flowers. It does best in full sun.*

Rudbeckia

ASTERACEAE/COMPOSITAE

Coneflower

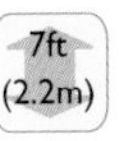

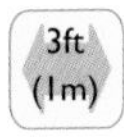

There are some 15 species in this genus, a mixture of annuals, biennials and perennials. They originate in moist woodlands in North America and flower over a long period from summer to autumn.

Many cultivars have been bred, and among them are some really large performers, the flowers of which are held aloft on long, slender stems. One of these is a cultivar of the rhizomatous cutleafed coneflower (*Rudbeckia laciniata* 'Hortensia' syn *R. l.* 'Golden Glow'). It is vigorous and tall, growing up to 6ft (1.8m), and bears fully double, yellow flowers with reflexed (turned back) petals with a greenish-yellow cone from midsummer to mid-autumn.

Another form to look out for is the hybrid *R.* 'Herbstsonne', which can grow up to 7ft (2.2m) tall. It has long, oval, toothed and prominently veined leaves that are up to 6in (15cm) long and bright yellow, single flowers, up to 5in (12cm) across, which are borne on branching stems.

WHERE TO PLANT

Coneflowers will grow in full sun or partial shade in moist soil. They will cope with heavy soil but will not tolerate drought, although most prefer drier conditions if they are grown in partial shade. If the soil is fertile, coneflowers can become invasive.

PLANT CARE

These sturdy plants do not normally require staking or much attention. Sow seeds in spring or divide clumps in autumn or spring. Slugs can be a problem with young shoots and leaves, and *R. laciniata* 'Hortensia' is susceptible to aphids.

PLANTING SUGGESTIONS

Grow coneflowers in a natural border in a damp area of the garden. They look best when they are planted in large, natural-looking drifts.

Rudbeckias are characterized by their daisy-like flowers, usually in yellow with a distinctive cone-shaped central boss (hence the common name). Most make good cut flowers.

Salvia

LABIATAE/LAMIACEAE

Sage

This huge and amazingly diverse genus includes a range of annuals, biennials, herbaceous and evergreen perennials, and shrubs, and a few of the perennials can certainly be described as giant while some others are decidedly large.

Azure blue sage (*Salvia azurea*, syn. *S. angustifolia*) is one of them. A woody-based perennial, it will grow to about 6ft (1.8m) high in the right conditions. It has sparsely branching stems with slender, fairly small, mid- to deep green leaves. From late summer to autumn the typical sage flowers (two lipped, the upper lip hooded) are borne in dense spires at the end of the flowering stems in white or blue.

Sapphire sage (*S. guaranitica*) (zones 9–10) is a subshrubby perennial, growing to about 5ft (1.5m) tall. It has slightly longer, hairy, mid-green leaves, and from midsummer to autumn it bears intense deep blue flowers, each 2in (5cm) long and with a purplish-blue calyx. *S. guaranitica* 'Black and Blue' is even taller, to 8ft (2.5m), and has darker blue flowers with purplish-blue calyces.

Bog sage (*S. uliginosa*) (zones 8–9) thrives in damp conditions, as its name suggests. It is a clump-forming, rhizomatous perennial with lance-shaped, deeply toothed leaves that are smaller as they emerge up the stems. From late summer to mid-autumn, small, light blue flowers are carried in spires that rise to a height of 6ft (1.8m).

WHERE TO PLANT

Different sages demand different conditions. Azure blue sage and sapphire sage will do best in light, humus-rich soil in full sun or dappled shade, but bog sage needs much moister soil. All do best if protected from cold, drying winds.

PLANT CARE

Sow seeds or divide clumps in spring. Alternatively, propagate sages from softwood cuttings in early summer. Young shoots and leaves are often attacked by slugs and snails, as are the rhizomes of bog sage.

*Sapphire sage (*Salvia guaranitica*), with its brilliant blue flowers, is taller than clary sage (right).*

PLANTING SUGGESTIONS

Grow azure blue sage and sapphire sage in a border based on pastel shades, such as blue, mauve, pink and soft purple, alongside lavender (*Lavandula*), wormwood (*Artemisia*), ornamental onions (*Allium*), bellflowers (*Campanula*) and phlox (*Phlox*). The slightly shorter biennial clary (*S. sclarea* var. *turkestanica*) is an erect plant, about 4ft (1.2m) tall, and its long leaves and clusters of pinkish-white flowers from spring to summer will lengthen the flowering season of the other sages. The flowers of many sages are attractive to bees, so they are often grown in wild gardens. Bog sage, however, should be grown in a bog garden or very damp soil.

*The biennial clary sage (*Salvia sclarea *var.* turkestanica*) is not the biggest of the sages, but with its pink and white flowers, it is certainly a garden-worthy large perennial.*

Sanguisorba

ROSACEAE

Bloodroot, Burnet

There are some 10 species in the genus, but only a few can be classed as giants. Canadian burnet (*Sanguisorba canadensis*), a spreading, clump-forming plant, is one of the largest of these rhizomatous perennials, which come from the temperate regions of the Northern Hemisphere. The most distinctive feature is the poker-like cone of green buds, which open in summer to form long, bottlebrush-like spikes of small white flowers. The hairy leaves are 10in (25cm) long, each one made up of up to 17 leaflets.

Although *S. officinalis* is known as great burnet, it grows only about 4ft (1.2m) tall. However, the cultivar *S. officinalis* 'Arnhem' can reach 7ft (2.2m). It has rich, glowing red spikes of flowers, which rise high above the basal leaves.

S. tenuifolia is another large species, and the cultivar *S. tenuifolia* 'Alba' forms delicate clumps of light green foliage in spring and graceful, small, white flower spikes on wiry stems.

WHERE TO PLANT

Grow in sun or partial shade in moist, fertile soil, which should be well-drained but never dried out.

PLANT CARE

You may need to stake the really big burnets to keep them upright, especially in less sheltered situations. They can become invasive, so divide clumps every spring or autumn. You can propagate them from seeds sown in spring or autumn or from divisions. Although slugs can damage young leaves, the plants are otherwise tough and trouble free.

PLANTING SUGGESTIONS

Plant burnets in a natural border with other big perennials, such as coneflowers (*Rudbeckia*), meadow rue (*Thalictrum*), aruncus and King Solomon's seal (*Polygonatum*).

Sanguisorbas are useful plants for the late summer border, and look good grown with grasses.

Solidago

ASTERACEAE/COMPOSITAE

Goldenrod

There are more than 100 species of woody-based perennials in this worthwhile genus, most of them originating in North America. Only one is a widely grown large goldenrod, *Solidago* 'Golden Wings'—the other cultivars tend to be half the size.

S. 'Golden Wings' has the usual stiffly branched stems with alternate, lance-shaped, mid-green leaves. The flowers, which bloom from late summer to early autumn, make a dramatic statement, reaching a height of up to 6ft (1.8m). They are borne in spires up to 10in (25cm) long at the tips of the branching stems and are a rich golden-yellow. They make good cut flowers, too.

WHERE TO PLANT

Grow goldenrod in a sunny position in poor or only moderately fertile soil; they do best in sandy soil, as they prefer freely draining ground.

PLANT CARE

These plants can be invasive, so it is best to remove the flowering stems before they set seeds. Goldenrod make sturdy clumps, which do not require staking despite being tall. Propagation should not normally be a problem, and you can divide the clumps in spring or autumn. They are normally fairly trouble-free, although powdery mildew might be a problem.

PLANTING SUGGESTIONS

Goldenrod looks wonderful planted with kniphofias, thistles (*Echinops*), mulleins (*Verbascum*) and fennel (*Foeniculum*) in a golden-, orange- or red-themed border. Alternatively, plant in drifts in a wild or natural garden, where the flowers attract large numbers of beneficial insects such as bees and butterflies.

Goldenrods spread quickly to form impressive drifts, and are at their best in late summer and early autumn when flowering.

Telekia speciosa

ASTERACEAE/COMPOSITAE

Ox eye daisy

In the wild, ox eye daisy (*Telekia speciosa*, formerly known as *Buphthalmum speciosum*) is found in moist woodlands and beside streams in central and southern Europe. It is a strikingly large, rhizomatous perennial, producing golden-yellow, daisylike flowers over a long season from early summer to early autumn. The flowers are composed of long, narrow petals around a central eye, which is surrounded by rows of overlapping bracts (modified leaves). The basal leaves are mid-green, oval and toothed at the edges, with long stalks. Smaller leaves are positioned alternately up the stems.

WHERE TO PLANT

Grow ox eye daisies in a sheltered, slightly shady spot in moist soil. They prefer slightly poor soil, so do not add too much fertilizer.

PLANT CARE

The plants self-seed easily, but if you wish to propagate them, grow from seeds sown in autumn. Divide existing clumps in spring. Ox eye daisies are generally trouble free, although slugs may be problematic as they attack young shoots.

PLANTING SUGGESTIONS

Ox eye daisies can be grown as specimen plants next to a natural pool. They are also ideal for damp woodland gardens or wild gardens, where they can be grown with a close cousin, *Buphthalmum salicifolium*, which has willow-like leaves and similar yellow flowers but is only half the height of *Telekia speciosa*. Both do well as cut flowers, as they are long lasting.

*The popular ox eye daisy (*Telekia speciosa*) will rapidly colonize poor soil.*

Thalictrum

RANUNCULACEAE

Meadow rue

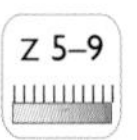

Found by streams and in damp meadows in the Northern Hemisphere, the rhizomatous and tuberous perennials in this genus are primarily shade-loving plants. They are grown for their slightly waxy foliage and for their fluffy flowers, which can be white or in shades of pink, mauve and yellow, and there are several really large back-of-the-border plants.

Thalictrum chelidonii is an erect, clump-forming rhizomatous perennial with long, divided leaves and clusters of mauve flowers with prominent yellow stamens at the tips of the flowering stems in late summer and early autumn. Originating from the Himalayas, this species prefers cool, damp summers, when it will grow to 8ft (2.5m).

Chinese meadow rue (*T. delavayi*) is smaller at 5ft (1.5m), but it, too, is a handsome plant with great clusters of fluffy lilac flowers with yellow stamens, borne from midsummer to early autumn.

WHERE TO PLANT

Meadow rues need humus-rich, moist soil in partial shade.

PLANT CARE

You will need to stake meadow rues to prevent them from flopping over. Ideally, divide and replant clumps every three years to maintain vigor. Because they can be late starting into growth in spring, take care that you do not damage the crowns (or dig them up) when you are planting or weeding the border. Slugs can damage young shoots, and powdery mildew is a problem if conditions are dry.

PLANTING SUGGESTIONS

Plant meadow rue at the back of a shady border with other moist shade-lovers, such as hostas (*Hosta*) and plume poppies (*Macleaya*).

Thalictrum *(meadow rue) comes in various forms. This variety (*Thalictrum aquilegifoliu *var.* Album*) is a pure white one, with aquilegia-like foliage.*

Veratrum

LILIACEAE/MELIANTHIACEAE

False hellebore

There are about 20 species in this genus of imposing perennials. The most garden-worthy, which are also impressively tall, are false (or white) hellebore (*Veratrum album*), American false hellebore (*V. viride*) and the black hellebore (*V. nigrum*). False hellebore has long oval leaves with a pleated appearance. The leaves are arranged in a cluster around the flowering stem, which bears branching spires, up to 2ft (60cm) long, of greenish-white, star-shaped flowers in early and midsummer.

American false hellebore, which is also called Indian poke, comes from North America. It has similar foliage to its European cousin and a broadly similar flowering habit and season, except that the flowers are green to greenish-yellow. The black hellebore (*V. nigrum*) is slightly smaller and copes with slightly cooler climates (zones 4–8). It blooms later, from mid- to late summer, bearing similar spires of deep reddish-brown flowers.

All parts of all false hellebores are poisonous, and the foliage can cause skin allergies, so take care when handling.

WHERE TO PLANT

Grow hellebore in deep, rich, slightly acid, moist soil in partial shade; they can be grown in sun if the soil never dries out. American false hellebore prefers even moister conditions. Shelter plants from cold, drying winds.

PLANT CARE

These erect plants do not need staking. Add bulky organic matter to the soil at planting time, because false hellebores are greedy feeders. Propagate by sowing seeds in spring or dividing plants in autumn or spring.

PLANTING SUGGESTIONS

Plant in a shady border or in a woodland garden.

Veratrum *(false hellebore) does best in moist, shady borders.*

Verbascum

SCROPHULARIACEAE

Mullein

The genus has more than 360 species, most of which are biennials, but some are perennials. Only two species, however that can be described as "giant,": *Verbascum bombyciferum* (syn. *V. broussa*) and candelabra mullein (*V. olympicum*) (syn. *V. longifolium*) are widely grown, and they are broadly similar in appearance. They have large rosettes of basal semi-evergreen or evergreen leaves, silver in color. In summer, felted and branching spires of yellow flowers sit on erect, sparsely branched spikes. *V. bombyciferum* can grow to 7ft (2.2m); candelabra mullein will reach 6ft (1.8m). Although they are grown for their magnificent spires of golden-yellow flowers, the silvery leaves are a prized feature in the winter garden. The species of *V. bombyciferum* and candelabra mullein are widely grown, but the cultivar *V.* 'Silver Lining' is popular and has particularly prominent silvery white foliage. Another species, common mullein (*V. thapsus*), grows to about 5ft (1.5m), although in the right conditions it will get to 6ft (1.8m). It is similar in appearance to the species described above.

WHERE TO PLANT

Plant in a sunny position in alkaline soil. Mulleins cope with poor soil provided it is well drained. They do extremely well in gravel gardens and will cope with a considerable degree of drought.

PLANT CARE

Despite their height, these tough, strong plants generally need no staking, but if they are grown in lush, fertile conditions, the stems will be sappier and may need support. Propagate by taking root cuttings in winter. Mildew is likely to be the main problem, and mulleins can also be attacked by moth caterpillars.

PLANTING SUGGESTIONS

Grow mulleins toward the back of a large mixed border, or naturalize in a wildflower garden.

There are several species of Verbascum *(mullein), which have impressive spires of yellow flowers.* V. bombyciferum *(right) is the biggest.*

Verbena

VERBENACEAE

Verbena

This genus contains a huge range of plant types, from tiny annuals to subshrubs, but almost all originate in the tropical and temperate regions of the North and South American continents, although a few come from southern Europe.

A notable giant and an imposing addition to a border, verbena Buenos Aires (*Verbena bonariensis*) (zones 7–11) is native to Brazil and Argentina. It has dark stems and many branching, flowering stems; the flowers, which are a brilliant lilac-purple, are borne at the tips in tight clusters, from midsummer to early autumn.

V. corymbosa is a rather similar perennial that grows from a rhizome. It produces large clusters of reddish-purple flowers. The leaves, like those of purple verbena, are toothed and slightly rough, but those of *V. corymbosa* are twice as large.

Swamp verbena (*V. hastata*) (zones 3–7) is similar to the other species but at 5ft (1.5m) is smaller. It usually bears violet to pinkish-purple flowers, but occasionally white flowers are produced.

WHERE TO PLANt

Grow verbenas in moderately fertile, well-drained soil in full sun. Provide some protection from cold, drying winds.

PLANT CARE

In colder areas these plants benefit from a thick dry mulch in winter; in coldest areas they will grow as annuals. Although the stems tend to flop slightly, staking is not really necessary because this lax habit is part of their charm. Propagate from seed sown in autumn or early spring, or divide plants in spring. You can also take stem cuttings in late summer. They are susceptible to a number of pests, notably aphids and thrips, and leafhoppers and slugs can also be a problem. Verbenas are often affected by powdery mildew.

Verbenas come in many forms. Purple verbena (V. bonariensis), opposite, is a giant, and it makes a great addition to a late summer border.

PLANTING SUGGESTIONS

Grow verbenas as part of a border with other pink-, mauve-, and blue-flowered plants, or in a smaller bed on their own as a feature, ideally against a west-facing light for best effects.

Vernonia

ASTERACEAE/COMPOSITAE

Ironweed

There are more than 1,000 species in this genus, but only the perennials are cultivated. Of these, *Vernonia noveboracensis* and *V. crinita* are most often found in gardens.

V. noveborancesis, which originates in the eastern United States, is an herbaceous perennial with branching stems clothed with lance-shaped, toothed leaves and, from late summer to mid-autumn, flat clusters of pinkish-purple heads of small, tubular flowers that have a fluffy appearance.

V. crinita (syn. *V. arkansana*) has tall stems topped with clusters of reddish-brown flowers from late summer to autumn. The taller cultivar *V. crinita* 'Mammuth' has delightful, rich violet-purple, aster-like flowers held aloft on stems that can be up to 8ft (2.5m) tall.

WHERE TO PLANT

Ironweeds prefer light, moderately fertile soil and will grow quite happily in either full sun or partial shade.

PLANT CARE

These plants do not normally need staking, but regular deadheading will help to prolong the flowering season. Divide clumps in spring or autumn to control vigor. New plants can be propagated from divisions or from seeds sown in spring. They are generally trouble-free.

PLANTING SUGGESTIONS

Plant in a wild garden or in a mixed border to extend the flowering season.

Vernonia crinita *(ironweed) is another good late-summer perennial for the back of the border.*

Veronicastrum virginicum

SCROPHULARIACEAE

Culver's root

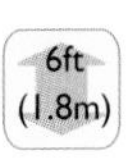

Originating from the meadows and prairies of North America and Siberia, there are two imposing herbaceous perennials in this genus, but the species *Veronicastrum virginicum* is more commonly grown in gardens.

The leaves of Culver's root (*Veronicastrum virginicum*, syn. *Veronica virginica*) are dark green, elongated, and toothed, and borne in whorls of five to seven leaflets up the stem of the plant. There are some good garden selections, including *V. virginicum* f. *album*, which has white flower spikes and gray-green leaves; *V. virginicum* 'Fascination', which is slightly smaller at 5ft (1.5m) but bears long spikes of lovely pinkish-mauve flowers; and *V. virginicum* 'Lavendelturm', which has lavender-blue flowers and grows to 6ft (1.8m) tall.

WHERE TO PLANT

Grow in moist but well-drained soil in full sun or partial shade. Do not let the soil dry out.

PLANT CARE

These stately plants do not normally need staking. Divide the plants in spring to control their spread and for propagation purposes. You can also take stem cuttings in early or midsummer. They are susceptible to mildews and leaf spot but are not generally affected by garden pests.

PLANTING SUGGESTIONS

Grow at the back of a border for height, with, for example, burnet (*Sanguisorba*) and colewort (*Crambe cordifolia*).

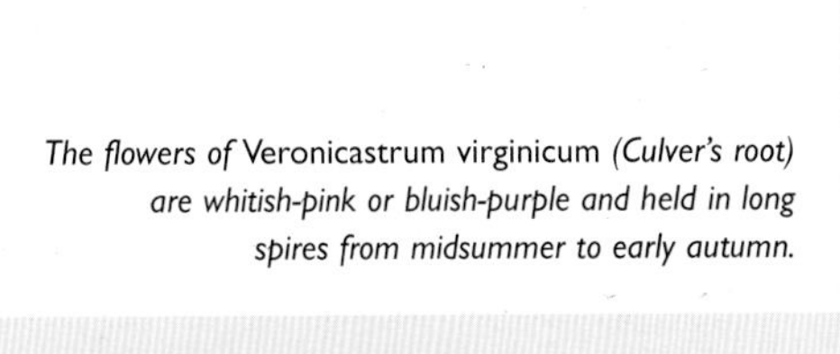

The flowers of Veronicastrum virginicum *(Culver's root) are whitish-pink or bluish-purple and held in long spires from midsummer to early autumn.*

Yucca

AGAVACEAE

Yucca

These woody, evergreen perennials from North America make very handsome architectural plants, with their large rosettes of long, leathery, sword-like leaves. They grow from a branched tap-root and produce tall spires of white flowers in summer.

Adam's needle (*Yucca filamentosa*) (zones 5–10) has leaves that can be 3ft (1m) long and are bluish-green in color. In summer it will produce a tall spire of white, bell-like flowers to 10ft (3m) or more high. *Yucca filamentosa* 'Bright Edge' (zones 6–10) has yellow-variegated leaves.

Spanish dagger (*Y. gloriosa*) is more tender (zones 7–10). It has a stout trunk that bears tufts of stiffly pointed leaves that start bluish-green and mature to darker green. From late summer, bell-shaped, white flowers with a purplish tinge rise above the leaves in an upright spike to a height of 8ft (2.5m) or so. *Yucca gloriosa* 'Nobilis' has bluish-green leaves in which the outer leaves of the rosette arch; *Y. gloriosa* 'Variegata' has yellow-margined leaves.

The hardy pendulous yucca (*Y. recurvifolia*) (zones 5–10) produces several trunk-like stems bearing arching mid-green leaves with toothed margins. The cream flowers are borne in spires up to 6ft (1.8m) long.

WHERE TO PLANT

Yuccas need well-drained soil and a position in full sun.

PLANT CARE

Easy to grow, yuccas need little attention and are able to withstand drought well. If you want the flowers to set seed, you may need to pollinate them by hand, but yuccas are best propagated from root cuttings taken in winter or by removing and planting rooted suckers in spring.

Yucca flacinda *is deservedly popular, its white spires of flowers rising high above many other plants in the garden in late summer.*

Remove the flowering stems once they wither, as they look unsightly.

PLANTING SUGGESTIONS

Yuccas are often grown as architectural features in eye-catching positions or as the largest features in an island bed. In colder areas, they can be grown in containers that can be protected with bubblewrap in winter or brought into a greenhouse.

This variety of Yucca filamentosa *has attractive, yellow-variegated leaves and a tall spire of white flowers.*

Index

Page numbers in italics refer to illustrations

Noxious plants

The plants listed below are banned in the following American states and Canadian provinces. Some areas will impose penalties, so contact your state or regional agriculture or plant extension office for additional information.

Allium spp are banned as noxious plants in Arkansas.
Angelica sylvestris is a problem plant in New Brunswick and possibly Quebec.
Cynara cardunculus is banned as a noxious plant in California.
Euphorbia spp plants are problems in the southern Prairie Provinces and southwestern Ontario.
Galega officinalis is banned as a noxious plant in Nevada and Pennsylvania.
Iris pseudacorus is a problem plant in southwestern Ontario.
Lysimachia nummularia is a problem plant across eastern Canada and British Columbia.
Miscanthus floridulus is banned as a noxious plant in Hawaii.
Onopordum acanthium is banned as a noxious plant in Arizona, California, Colorado, Idaho and Missouri.
Salvia sclarea is banned as a noxious plant in Washington.
Verbascum thapsus is a problem plant in some Ontario areas.

Acknowledgments

Photographs on the following pages are copyright ©:
Jonathan Buckley 64.
Chris Burrows/The Garden Picture Library 55.
Collins & Brown 32–33.
Eric Crichton/The Garden Picture Library 44.
John Glover/The Garden Picture Library 45, 89.
Carole Ottesen/Garden IMAGE 58.
Howard Rice 113.
Harry Smith Collection 46, 51, 52, 54, 57, 61, 70, 72,74, 85, 91, 96, 98, 103, 110, 114, 123,124, 125, 127, 128–129, 136.
Steve Wooster All jacket pictures. 6–7, 7,8–9 (Great Dixter), 10–11, 11, 12 (Butterstream), 13, 14 (The Beth Chatto Gardens), 15l (The Beth Chatto Gardens),15r, 16 (Annes Grove), 17t (Pridna Gardens), 17b (Winter Garden), 18, 18–19 (The Beth Chatto Gardens), 20 (Great Dixter), 21 (The Beth Chatto Gardens), 22–23,23b (Glebe Cottage Plants), 24–25, 25 (Creagh Gardens), 26, 27t, 27b, 28,29 (Hampton Court), 30–31 (Great Dixter), 42–43 (The Beth Chatto Gardens), 47, 48 (The Beth Chatto Gardens), 49 (The Beth Chatto Gardens), 50 (The Beth Chatto Gardens), 53 (The Beth Chatto Gardens),56 (The Beth Chatto Gardens), 59, 60 (Craigholm), 62 (Ilford Manor), 63 (Burford House Gardens),65 (The Beth Chatto Gardens), 66 (The Beth Chatto Gardens), 67 (The Beth Chatto Gardens), 68, 69, 71, 73 (Wisley), 75, 76,77 (The Beth Chatto Gardens), 78 (The Beth Chatto Gardens), 79 (The Beth Chatto Gardens), 80 (The Beth Chatto Gardens), 81 (The Beth Chatto Gardens), 82, 83 (The Beth Chatto Gardens), 84 (The Beth Chatto Gardens), 86 (The Beth Chatto Gardens),87, 88, 90, 92 (The Beth Chatto Gardens), 93 (The Beth Chatto Gardens), 95 (Gethsemane Garden),97, 99, 100 (The Beth Chatto Gardens), 101, 102 (Mien Ruys Garden), 104, 105 (The Beth Chatto Gardens),106 (Butterstream), 107, 108, 109 (Andrew Kearny's Garden), 111, 112 (Hampton Court), 115 (The Beth Chatto Gardens), 116 (The Beth Chatto Gardens), 117 (The Beth Chatto Gardens), 118 (The Beth Chatto Gardens), 119 (The Beth Chatto Gardens), 120 (Great Dixter),121, 122 (Diana Firth's garden), 126, 130 (The Beth Chatto Gardens),131 (The Beth Chatto Gardens), 132 (The Beth Chatto Gardens), 133 (The Beth Chatto Gardens),134 (The Beth Chatto Gardens), 135,137, 138 (The Beth Chatto Gardens), 139.

Zone Map of the U.S. and Canada

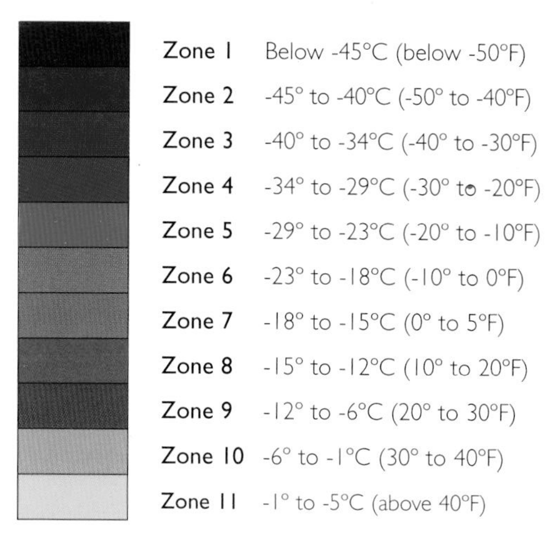

A plant's winter hardiness is critical in deciding whether it is suitable for your garden. The map below divides the United States and Canada into 11 climactic zones based on average minimum temperatures, as compiled by the U.S. Department of Agriculture. Find your zone and check the zone information in the plant directory to help you choose the plants most likely to flourish in your climate.